CLEARING

AWAY

CLOUDS

CLEARING

AWAY

CLOUDS

Nine Lessons

for Life

from the

Martial Arts

STEPHEN FABIAN

First edition, 1999

04   03   02   01   00   99   6   5   4   3   2   1

Library of Congress Cataloging-in-Publication Data
    Clearing away clouds : nine lessons for life from the martial arts /
    Stephen Fabian. -- 1st ed.
        p.   cm.
    Includes bibliographical references.
    ISBN 0-8348-0468-9
    1. Martial arts--Psychological aspects. 2. Martial arts--Philosophy. 3. Conduct of
life. I. Title
GV1102.7.P75F33   1999
796.8--dc21   99-27532
                                                  CIP

To my parents,

Irene Esther Sawka Fabian

and (the late) Paul Peter Fabian,

whose love gave me life,

and whose example gives me

a model for living.

CONTENTS

ACKNOWLEDGMENTS

Perhaps the most enjoyable and yet difficult part of any book to write is this section in which the author gladly acknowledges all known and remembered contributors to the work, hoping to slight no one in the process. For this book the task is especially daunting, since the path of my personal development has enjoyed the benefit of so many contributors, it would be impossible to mention them all here, even if I still could remember all of them.

Since the work focuses on my martial development, I'll begin by recognizing my various teachers, including Yager Sensei, Mr. Arthur Chan, and Master Nam Kwon Hyong and his brother Namsoo Hyong Sabeom. These men all contributed greatly to my early martial and personal development. In Japan, Master Inoue Tsuyoshi Munetoshi, 18th Soke, or headmaster, of the Hontai Yoshin Ryu, continues to be a model, guide, and inspiration. Other *honbu dojo* teachers include Inoue Kyoichi Sensei, as well as Mitsuyasu Sensei, Sato Sensei, Kanazawa Sensei, Yasumoto Sensei, and (the late) Kurushima Sensei. They have been most ably helped by senior students, my *senpai*, including Hikari-san, Nakai-san, Negoro-san, and Sato-san. And several of my own students have contributed significantly to my development, including Brian Barnes, Stephen Sawyer, Todd Schweinhart, and John Sims. To all of the above and all fellow students of Hontai Yoshin Ryu, I owe not only deep gratitude and respect, but an obligation as well to continue to teach and live in accordance with what I have been taught.

My martial development has paralleled other facets of personal development, especially in the area of academics. Here, I must thank two men who have been particularly instrumental in my intellectual growth, as well as enriching me with powerful personal models of life and achievement: Anthony F. Aveni of Colgate University, and R. Tom Zuidema of the University of Illinois at Urbana-Champaign. In addition, anthropologist Ginger Farrer has long been a close friend and mentor, a true elder in the best tradition of this term, and I thank her also for her many kindnesses and unselfish sharing of time, information, and advice.

While preparing this manuscript, I was helped considerably by friends and colleagues who read and commented on the work in progress: John Ahrens, Hugh E. Davey, Wayne Muromoto, and Nicklaus Suino. Ray Furse, editorial director of Weatherhill, has also provided necessary guidance in the content and technicalities of the manuscript. To them goes much of the credit and none of the blame for the text that follows.

My family has been ever supportive of my martial and other personal endeavors, even when it has meant sacrifice on their parts. Sincere thanks to my children—Rebecca, Julia, and Alexander—for their patience and understanding during the considerable time I spend away from them, and their enthusiastic interest in my martial activities. I cannot thank my wife Surabela adequately for her efforts on my behalf—including reading and commenting on an earlier version of this manuscript—and her sharing of my Way. The constant encouragement of my brother Paul is a strong source of strength for me, as well; for this and his intelligent and thoughtful comments on the text, my gratitude.

Ultimately, as much as I owe to so many, my greatest debt of gratitude and obligation is to my parents, Irene and (the late) Paul Fabian. Tireless in their efforts to raise me and in their own way masters of full and humble living, theirs is a model I can only hope to continue to strive toward. It is to them that I very respectfully dedicate this book.

CLEARING
AWAY
CLOUDS

INTRODUCTION

Warriors learn military science accurately
and go on to practice the techniques of martial arts diligently.
The way that is practiced by warriors is not obscure in the
least. Without any confusion in mind, without slacking off at
any time, polishing the mind and attention, sharpening the eye
that observes and the eye that sees, one should know real
emptiness as the state where there is no obscurity and the
clouds of confusion have cleared away.

—Miyamoto Musashi, *The Book of Five Rings*

To be able to live and function without confusion— how
appealing in this fast-paced modern world, with its plethora of
ethical dilemmas, overwhelming flow of new information, and
emphasis on individual choice and satisfaction. In such a
world, dare we hope to possess the clarity of vision and purpose that would allow us to tread confidently and securely? Is
such a life really possible? How can it be achieved?

Miyamoto Musashi (1584–1645), author of the above quote
and Japan's most famous master swordsman, knew such clarity of mind, and applied it successfully during a life of combative self-exploration, artistic expression, and training in his
chosen vocation, which he called "the way of strategy."
Musashi lived through the end of a turbulent feudal epoch
marked by incessant warfare and into the early and restless
years of a relatively peaceful period established by the
Tokugawa *shogun*, or chief military leaders, that was to last
over two centuries. For the *bushi*, or samurai warriors, like
Musashi, it was a time of challenge, requiring a shift from the
combat duties of obligatory feudal service to the administra-
tion of peace.

Although verifiable historical details on Musashi are fragmentary, he is known as Kensei, or Sword Saint, in Japan, having survived by his own account over sixty *shinken shobu*, duels to the death, and creating his famous two-sword fighting style, Niten Ichi Ryu. Martial artist extraordinaire, Musashi also trained himself in such creative and peaceful arts as painting, sculpture, and calligraphy, producing masterpieces of international renown. As warrior, artist, and author, Musashi led a life of rarely equaled intensity and talent, a life in which mastery—of the arts as well as the self—was actualized through a profound clarity of mind, one from which all obscuring clouds had been cleared away.

While Musashi may have been extraordinary, the arts he practiced were not. From long before Musashi's time right up until today countless Japanese and other Asians, and increasingly those neither Japanese nor Asian, have been practicing these same arts, using them not only as a means of creative expression or self-defense, but as paths of personal development. It is the process of this personal development that in fact enables mastery of form and technique, which in turn allows further mastery of self.

If deftly manipulating the tea-server's whisk, the calligrapher's brush, or the warrior's sword can all lead to and exemplify mastery, then, with due regard to the considerable differences in tools and techniques, there must be some essential characteristics shared by these arts. By looking beyond or beneath specific styles, we should be able to discern some shared, underlying principles, the essence of what has come to be translated as the "Way." This is a concept that hearkens from the ancient Chinese philosophy of Taoism and its early and most famous expression in Lao Tzu's *Tao Te Ching.* The term *tao* (in Chinese pronounced as the "Dow" of Dow-Jones) and *do* (in Japanese pronounced like "dough") are written with the Chinese ideogram for "road." Appending this term to refer to specific arts, such as *sado,* the "way of tea," or *budo,* the "martial way," indicates that they are as well paths for the development of the self toward a state of pure, unfeigned, and naturally harmonious existence. They are means to attain mastery, a Way.

True mastery either of ourselves or any artistic pursuit comparable to the level attained by Musashi may not be within the grasp of us all. But how can we know until we try, and wouldn't we all be better for the effort? Knowing the principles on which the ways of mastery are based could help us see the Way more clearly. From my own experience of over twenty years following the martial path, and with the help of teachers, those senior to me, *senpai*, and students whom I have known personally or whose work I have read, comes this presentation of principles of the Way, a logical progression that can guide one along the road to martial and self-mastery. I consider them, as the subtitle of this book suggests, Nine Lessons for Life from the Martial Arts. Briefly, they are:

1. Embrace a Way
2. Accept responsibility for your actions
3. Control the breath
4. Focus
5. Develop self-discipline
6. Train hard, seeking aesthetic refinement
7. Be patient and flow
8. Persevere
9. Cultivate the mind of no-mind

I am convinced that all seekers of mastery eventually discover these same principles, learn these same lessons. The order in which I list and describe them is as much an organizational device as it is a record of personal experience. Once you have embraced your Way, all of these lessons will be active and interactive throughout your quest for mastery; how and when you become aware of their relevance to your progress may differ in order and intensity. It is also quite feasible to achieve mastery with no conscious awareness of these principles at all, just as we can breathe fresh air without knowing its chemical properties or understanding the mechanics of breathing.

MASTERY OF AND THROUGH THE MARTIAL ARTS

Surviving a battle depends upon maintaining a state of mind unaffected by external factors or internal weakness; thus the connection between self-mastery and martial prowess is an old, strong, and logical one. A sincere study of a traditional East Asian martial system under enlightened guidance has much to offer. Just as Musashi emphasized in his own life and in his treatise on the Way of martial strategy, there are few undertakings that can compare favorably with what a properly conducted martial system has to offer you for personal development.

Although it may seem contradictory that arts or skills designed for killing can be used for self-improvement, the seeming paradox is resolved via the Eastern experience of recognizing and using the weapons and ways of destruction—the life-taking sword—to be the fundamental tools and means of perfecting valued human qualities—the life-giving sword. This has been possible particularly in the East, where the doctrines of Confucianism, Taoism, and Buddhism (and in Japan, Shinto) all place emphasis on positive personal development only within broader contexts of human society and the natural order of the cosmos.

Exactly when martial disciplines began to incorporate these more developmental, philosophical aspects is beyond the scope of this book. Certainly the contributions of Zen Buddhism, particularly to the Way of the Warrior in Japan, are especially noteworthy in this regard; both Zen and feudal militarism gained prominence in Japan at about the same time (ca. AD 1200). As D.T. Suzuki details in his essay on "Zen and the Samurai," in *Zen and Japanese Culture*, there are sound, natural reasons for this affiliation. Zen appealed morally and philosophically to the samurai because it "teaches us not to look backward once the course is decided upon, [and] because it treats life and death indifferently." The fact that Zen relies upon and develops intuition over intellection would also be attractive to warriors for whom active thought during the heat of combat actually may be life-threatening. In addition, Suzuki contends that "Zen discipline is simple, direct, self-reliant, self-denying," ascetic traits that go well with the "fighting spirit." Such emphases from Zen, when applied to the normal regimen of warrior training, produced fighters of superior quality.

This blend of warrior training with Zen guidance makes for a particularly effective path for achieving the personal growth and self-control that can lead one to mastery. The combination of intensive physical training, self-discipline, and overall mind-body control garnered via proper martial training is difficult to equal through any other single Way. The martial arts, when learned and practiced effectively and with the correct frame of mind, offer uniquely rich possibilities for mastery of technique, form, and self.

But beware the Warrior's Way. For many, the image conjured up by reference to "martial artists" is that of domineering ruffians, little more than disciplined bullies. It is the image of the Cobra Kai instructor from the *Karate Kid* films; the evil overlord against whom Bruce Lee is pitted in his famous *Enter the Dragon*; the vile villains against whom Chuck Norris so frequently battles. Even in Japan, where the combination of Zen and martial training have blossomed magnificently from their fecund cross-fertilization, the excesses of the Japanese military during its years of Asian-Pacific expansion have strongly tainted perceptions of the positive personal development possible through martial pursuits.

Admittedly, the same path that offers so much promise in the Way of self-mastery and enlightenment also offers the possibility of progress along the paths of self-aggrandizement, conceit, and egotism. On these paths, new and refined fighting abilities are used to promote personal agenda without regard for the impact this may have on others; power is cultivated for power's sake and "might makes right" is justified, if even considered, by a kind of Social Darwinism. Power itself can have a corrupting influence, so we should not be surprised to see

the all-too-human failings of greed, lust, and selfishness in a
martial artist, although it is always disappointing.

Unfortunately, a self-serving attitude can be implicitly
encouraged by otherwise talented and well-meaning instructors. A friend of mine who attended a major martial arts competition with hundreds in attendance tells that during the pro-
ceedings the master of ceremonies called for a certain Master
So-And-So to come forth. The announcement was repeated
without response. Finally, a black-belted student disengaged
himself from the rest of the crowd and spoke briefly with the
emcee. The next announcement was slightly altered: "Will
*Grand*master So-And-So please come forward." Sure enough,
this corrected paging did get a response. I am not suggesting
we should ignore the appropriate use of titles, but the example set by this instructor is one that will likely encourage student vanity. The instructor could have come forward and
humbly corrected the misspoken title, which would have sent
a clear message without appearing so insufferably egotistical.

Because martial training improves our physical abilities
and therefore supplies the impetus for feeling good about
ourselves, self-confidence will normally develop as well,
especially enhanced by a feeling, warranted or not, of being
able to "take care of" ourselves. Hence the appeal of the martial arts as programs for children, to inculcate such valuable
traits as positive self image and belief in themselves, as well
as self-defense skills. But if not properly balanced by the
enhancement of their humility, respect, etiquette, and feelings
of obligation to others, this confidence and positive self-
image can easily turn into conceit and domineering machis-
mo. Such development is antithetical to true mastery of self
and the finer qualities associated with those sincerely treading the Way.

ALTERNATIVES TO MARTIAL TRAINING

Although training in martial disciplines offers invaluable
opportunities for progress toward self-mastery and is the main
subject of this book, personal growth and mastery is also

achievable through many other endeavors. Noted in this regard are Japanese cultural arts such as *shodo*, or calligraphy, *chado (sado)*, or the tea ceremony, and *ikebana* or *kado*, the artful arrangement of flowers. Powerful examples of such mastery in a broad array of traditional Japanese arts is presented in a documentary made by the National Geographic Society in 1980, *Living Treasures of Japan*, which profiles a number of Japanese men and women who have been officially designated by the government as "Living National Treasures."

These masters demonstrate that virtually any traditional artistic or craft activity, from paper-making to theater, can provide a context for pursuing mastery. The master *bunraku* puppeteer Yoshida Tomao seems to speak for them all when he describes his work as the "artistry of revealing *hara* [physically located in the lower abdomen just below the navel], the inner center of emotion and spirit." Having been a puppeteer for about fifty years at the time the film was made, his formula for mastery was clear and simple: "From the day I started until today, every day has been training, discipline, learning. And it will be study and practice until the day I die."

Through intensive training, self-discipline, and the other steps presented in the nine lessons here, these artists have mastered their Ways and themselves. By so deeply involving their own inner beings in their art, they are able to poignantly touch the souls of others viewing or using their work. Hands, hearts, and minds have melded with the materials and actions with which they work daily to create true beauty, a beauty that also pervades their own being.

Developing the self via artistic expression according to Zen precepts is a fundamental and well-known path to self-mastery. But the Way to self-mastery does not require that a person be steeped in Oriental wisdom or Zen training. Other cultures around the world, Western and Eastern, have their own recognized and recognizable masters, men and women whose skill in specific activities is obvious and undeniable, as is their unflappable calm. Such individuals seem invariably to manifest an uncommon depth and strength of character: their power and talent is not only physical, but comes as a result of the coordination and effort of their total being in their chosen endeavor.

At times the specific activity, the Way leading to mastery, seems unlikely. Although some would see the competitive sport known as "bodybuilding" as an activity dominated by muscle-bound and narcissistic jocks, it is also an art form in which the human body becomes a medium for sculpting, an undertaking that requires tremendous discipline, perseverance, and motivation. Arnold Schwarzenneger, perhaps the world's most famous bodybuilder, has this to say in his autobiography *Arnold: The Education of a Bodybuilder:* "I think the most important things I developed through bodybuilding were my personality, confidence, and character." His road to fame (and fortune) was paved from the materials he used in his daily training regimen: "I taught myself discipline, the strictest kind of discipline . . . I could apply that discipline to everyday life." A seven-time winner of professional bodybuilding's most prestigious award, Mr. Olympia, Schwarzenneger also has been the number one international box office attraction, has served as the Chairman of the President's Council on Physical Fitness, and promotes the healthy development of inner city youth and the handicapped through various athletic programs he organizes and supports. For these successes he credits more his brain than his brawn: "You must consider that in the beginning you are training the mind as well as the body . . . The mind is incredible. Once you've gained mastery over it, channeling its powers *positively* for your purposes, you can do anything." Clearly, in mastering control over matter—whether clay, the implements of tea, flowers, or physical movements such as kicks and punches—mastery also can come over mind, heart, and spirit.

Ultimately, this is the Way of mastery: the enduring process of discovery and knowledge, applied in the forging of stronger and better technique, form, and self.

THE SWORD AND PEN ARE ONE

While the martial arts offer a particularly effective option for mastery, and while mastery is also achievable in other serious, artistic endeavors, fullest personal development is perhaps best achieved by some combination of the two. In Japanese there is an expression *Bunbu ryodo* (sometimes *Bunbu ryoho* or *Bunbu ichi*), which essentially means, "Cultural and martial [development] are both one Way," or more figuratively, "The sword and pen are one." Musashi echoes this expression early in the Earth Scroll chapter of his *Book of Five Rings:* "First of all, the way of warrior means familiarity with both cultural and martial arts." And Nitobe Inazo, in his work *Bushido,* tells us that part of the standard curriculum of the *bushi,* besides such martial disciplines as horsemanship, fencing, archery, jujutsu, and spearmanship, was the study of calligraphy, ethics, and literature.

As Musashi himself discovered, to develop as a total human being, martial valor and ferocity needs tempering with the sensitivity and softness more frequently associated with non-martial, creative arts. Conversely, the strength of spirit cultivated in the fighting arts can supply the boldness and dynamism that can bring vivid life to any art. This is the manifestation of the essential unity of the timeless dualities of yin and yang, neither of which is complete without the other.

My wish is that through reading this book, seekers of mastery will be able to apply its nine lessons to virtually any endeavor to which they seriously dedicate themselves. Once developed, the new knowledge, skills, awareness, and control that accompany sincere efforts at mastery can be applied to other dimensions of life. This effort to help seekers clear away clouds of confusion is my main purpose in writing this book. I also hope it will motivate and inspire, as other autobiographical works written by travelers of the martial Way have motivated and inspired me, works like Funakoshi Gichin's *Karate-Do: My Way of Life,* C.W. Nicol's *Moving Zen,* and Dave Lowry's *Autumn Lightning.* Such works are too few, and so I offer this book as a contribution, however unworthy, to the field.

I am also moved to share these lessons as part of the obligation and indebtedness I feel to the teachers, beginning with my parents, I have had along the Way. Knowing that there is no way to adequately repay what I have been given, I hope that writing this can serve at least in part as an expression of my gratitude to them for their teachings and other kindnesses, and a sharing of their wisdom with more people than they can personally reach. For as I hope to make clear by the end of the work, helping each other, acknowledging and acting on our social responsibilities, is really at the core of why we should bother at all about mastery. All of the effort we put into our own personal development is worth nothing if it isn't somehow put to use to benefit others.

EMBRACE A WAY

That the ideal mind might be achieved through swordsmanship derives from Buddhist, Confucian, and Taoist philosophies, which suggest implicitly or explicitly that the pursuit of any worthy endeavor leads to spiritual liberation. The pursuit can be anything: dancing, garden designing, tea drinking, sword brandishing. Once something is taken up and becomes a serious undertaking, it is called *michi* or *do* (*tao* in Chinese), the "Way." And mastering the Way means becoming enlightened.

—Hiroaki Sato, *The Sword and the Mind*

Since life and the Way of mastery is a process, when does it begin? Did I choose the martial Way for myself, or was I chosen for or by it? My own formal martial training began somewhat late, not until I was twenty and a college student. All of my grandparents were immigrants from Eastern Europe, and as a hot-tempered boy I knew nothing of Asian martial systems, neither as ways of fighting nor as a Way to enlightenment and self-mastery. But there were the glimmerings of the warrior . . .

I grew up on a small farm, the second of two sons in a blue-collar, upstate New York family. At harvest time, my brother and I would craft staffs and swords from sunflower stalks and spar and joust with great vigor. We also enjoyed archery, fashioning crude bows and arrows from saplings and string. My warrior's spirit was further kindled by Tolkien's magical trilogy *Lord of the Rings* before I was barely a teen, a fire I fed with other readings of warrior heroes, such as Robert E. Howard's *Conan,* Talbot Mundy's *Tros of Samothrace,* the heroes of Sir Walter Scott, and Tarzan and other larger than life figures of Edgar Rice Burroughs. Ladders and ropes, trees and barn lofts, forests and open meadows, all became my training ground.

Nor was I satisfied with solely physical development. I began to conceive of my physical body as a temple, housing a sacred presence and mystical force within. As an Eagle Scout, I was further inspired by the Boy Scout oath to keep myself "physically strong, mentally awake, and morally straight." I strove to balance training and awareness among the principal facets of self, conceptualized as mind, body, and spirit, but so intertwined as to be one. This early holistic training produced results that were recognized: on a warm evening in June, 1974, I graduated from high school as the scholar-athlete of my class.

Something also occurred while I was in my teens that opened my eyes to new possibilities, planting the seed of a new idea. This was the movie, later followed by the popular TV series, called *Kung Fu*, starring David Carradine as Caine, a Chinese-American orphan accepted into the famed Shaolin temple, the semi-mystical place credited by many as the birthplace of Zen-influenced martial arts. The story depicts Caine's growth from a naive and untrained child to a Shaolin monk, a master trained rigorously in philosophy, ethics, and the martial arts. In the idealized figure of the Shaolin monk—attuned to and at one with the universe, a lethal fighter who nevertheless preferred the way of harmony and peace—my own formative views of self began to crystallize. Here was self-control and total development of mind, body, and spirit, a warrior so skilled that he could choose the type and level of defense to apply: "Preserve rather than destroy; avoid rather than check; check rather than hurt; hurt rather than maim; maim rather than kill; for all life is precious, nor can any be replaced," as quoted in the introduction to the book *Kung Fu* by Chow and Spangler. Caine was a religious man who also had welded and forged his physical and mental being with the fires of hard training, long meditation, and ascetic living. The simplicity of lifestyle, practical effectiveness of technique, spiritual calm, and Eastern mysticism were all fascinating and inspirational.

Alas! This character was as fictional as any other who had impressed me in my youth; moreover, there was no Shaolin temple in upstate New York, nor was I aware of any school or system that offered anything remotely similar. But a dream image, a model, had formed.

Through a process of mutual selection, I decided to attend Colgate University, a private liberal arts institution with a reputation for academic excellence. As a first-generation college student, I had no idea as to a major field of study, nor any clear sense of what career I might want to pursue. The personal atmosphere of the small school seemed likely to be a good place to make these discoveries. But my entry was unpropitious. As soon as my brother and I had unloaded my few possessions in my dorm room, we were called into the Dean of Freshmen's office. Wondering what I could possibly have done wrong already, we sat down and received the unnerving news that since we had left home that morning, my father had died.

Although only sixty at the time of his death, my father had long suffered from arteriosclerosis and heart disease, and had in fact lived during my lifetime with only a third of his heart tissue functional. In spite of this, his was a robust presentation to the world. Strong and muscular, he was almost never idle, and even after being put on permanent disability was more often working around the yard and garden than sitting in the house. His strength and health had been noticeably failing throughout the summer prior to my departure, but his indomitable spirit, the never-say-die attitude with which he had lived every day of life as long as I had known him, did not allow any of us to think that his passing was imminent. His death on the very day that I, his younger son, was leaving home, now an adult on my own, sent a message that still leaves me with goosebumps, and a deep sense of wonder and awe. The message for me was that finally, with his family raised and cared for, his work in this earthly realm was complete. The strength of spirit that had supported him on borrowed time—his doctors had given him no hope twenty years earlier after his first heart attack—was now able to usher his soul to a new stage of existence. Although my father knew nothing of Eastern philosophy or martial arts, I have never seen his masterly warrior's example equaled.

Fortunately, Colgate was only about an hour's drive from home. Back we went, and when next I arrived at the university, I was already behind: no orientation, late for classes, and late for football tryouts. I was out of synch with the school, and struggling with myriad thoughts and emotions. Still, it was probably therapeutic to be as busy as I soon became. Attending classes, doing homework, daily football practice, all kept me from dwelling on myself and the gap created by my father's passing, coupled by my first experience living away from home.

In spite of my relative athletic success in high school, I found the level of competition at Colgate to be either beyond my abilities, or beyond my motivation. Standing five feet, ten inches and weighing about a hundred seventy-five pounds at the time, I was one of the smallest players on the football team, and once we freshmen began running plays against the varsity squad, as a substitute halfback I as often as not found myself at the bottom of a ton of bodies, picking sod from my face mask. And later in track, I soon found that a semi-rural all-county winner did not stack up very well against the quality of Colgate's foes.

I spent much of my first and only season of collegiate football on the injured list, and decided it would be my last. Afterwards, I competed in track and field for two years, but left that as well due to my own deficiencies and the dissatisfaction about where the activity was taking me in terms of personal development. In America we tend to focus, to our detriment, I believe, on competitive athletics for both physical and character development. My experience indicates that the efficacy of competitive athletics to achieve these goals—especially as they are generally practiced, with their overt emphasis on winning—is questionable and limited. Nevertheless, for many of us, not participating in interscholastic athletic competition leaves a gaping hole in our experience of life and self.

Fortunately, I found that other ways of athletic endeavor and development do exist.

FORMALLY EMBARKING ON THE WAY

Endings are also beginnings. The time I had been spending in formal practice for team sports now became my own again. I began to tailor my workouts more to my interests, blending some weight training with running and club gymnastics (which essentially meant dynamic calisthenics workouts). In addition, I was able to pick up again on speed-bag training, to which I had been introduced while in high school by my brother after his boxing lessons at West Point. I combined formal scheduling and cross-training in an instinctive regimen which helped heal old injuries and generally improved my physical, mental, and emotional condition.

Around this time a classmate asked me and several others if we would be interested in joining him in martial arts training. Arthur Chan was a Chinese-American from New York City's Chinatown, who had a black belt in Sikaran karate. After nearly two years without formal workouts, he was desperate to train, and he wanted his close friends to share his experience. The half dozen of us he asked all shared a vision of developing and melding our physical, mental, and spiritual capacities, and we were all excited by the prospect of training together in the martial arts. I distinctly remember the first time I put on my uniform, white top and hand-dyed black bottoms. It fit well and felt "right," and even our friend and teacher commented that I wore the uniform as if I already had worn it a long time, like a black belt. As it turned out, these were auspicious and prophetic words. My formal training along the Way of the Oriental warrior had begun, a path that I somehow already felt familiar with and embraced with wholeheartedness, and a way that I have now followed for more than two decades.

Our training was simple but hard. We had no formal training hall, but bringing life and our own interpretation to the late karate master Funakoshi Gichin's words "anyplace can be a *dojo* [training hall]," we trained outdoors, in the college wrestling room, in squash and racquetball courts, and even in our dorm rooms. Repetition of basics and abundant sweat were the common elements of our sessions, which included practice of closed- and open-handed strikes; front, side, and roundhouse kicks; low stances and simple combinations. New stretches improved flexibility, while soreness in new places was mitigated by sensations of physical growth and of the rightness of the training, of its fit with the core of my being.

Certainly not all of the training was "fun" for us, and for our teacher and friend it must at times have been utterly exasperating. None of us had trained martial arts before, and our movements were terribly clumsy and awkward, especially in the beginning. There were conflicts in scheduling, variations in physical aptitude, and differences in personality. We read books such as *Aikido and the Dynamic Sphere* for inspiration, and discussed our opinions on the internal, life-giving energy called *ki* (in Japanese) or *ch'i* (in Chinese) as well as the effectiveness of specific techniques, and the spiritual and mystical side of life and the martial arts. We began knuckle development with push-ups and a wall-mounted punching pad, and we practiced breaking techniques on a plastic break-away board.

One evening we sparred. Unfortunately, although we possessed at the time an over-abundance of strength and enthusiasm, we had no protective equipment, uncertain form, and poor control—a bad combination for sparring. As it happened, my face managed to drive itself onto the unpadded fist of my sparring partner, a friend and gymnast with pectorals so abundant that one of his high school sports teams had once given him a bra as a present. This stopped the bout, and in the restroom mirror I was able to make a preliminary assessment of the damage: my left cheek was red, the nose bleeding, and the left side of it oddly depressed. An X-ray at the college infirmary confirmed my suspicions: the nose where it attached to the cheek was broken, and surgery was recommended.

I demurred on the surgery and continued training gingerly, avoiding contact for awhile. But fate or karma had other plans;

several days later, while holding a target for our teacher, who was doing advanced combinations including back spinning kicks, I failed to move back far or fast enough. His techniques and control were excellent, and even though he came around blindly on this particular spinning kick, expecting me two feet further back, he deftly "pulled" his blow. His foot went whisking by my face, and his toes made only the slightest contact across my nose. There was a sharp, momentary pain at the site of my break. Again I went to the washroom, and once the involuntary flow of tears stopped, I was able to confirm with my eyes what my fingers were already telling me. Incredibly, my friend's kick had reset my nose and cheek connection, something the attending emergency room physician had informed me would be possible only with surgery. Deeply moved, our group was left to ponder the significance of this extraordinary occurrence.

BROADENING THE PATH

To complement our training, Arthur Chan suggested that we participate in the university's karate or self-defense classes. These met once a week, and were run by a man of impressive proportions whom we addressed as Sensei, a Japanese term of respect that is applied to teachers of all arts and disciplines. Slightly over six feet and broad shouldered, Sensei was an ex-Navy man with a mustache and graying, shoulder-length hair that he generally restrained with a headband. When we first met him, his well-worn black belt had three red stripes taped on it (a fourth was later added), and he represented an organization that was based upon Okinawan Goju Ryu karate. The style could be classified as a "hard" or "external" style, as there was considerable emphasis on conditioning the major outer striking surfaces of the body (knuckles, forearms, and shins). However, we also practiced the *sanchin kata* (one of the many standardized sets of movements called "forms," or *kata* in Japanese) which emphasized breath control and dynamic tension, as well as other methods effective in developing inner *ki* as well as raw external power.

Sensei was a powerful individual. Besides the dynamic and focused power obvious in the sharp execution of his *kata* and basic techniques, he also lifted weights, and his ability to coordinate his considerable mind-body energy became evident in the occasional demonstrations of board- and brick-breaking he would perform. It would have been easy to form a wrong impression of the man. Someone looking only superficially may have seen him as on some macho trip, a hard case who gloried in violence and the adoration of his intimidated followers. After all, his self-avowed philosophy about conflict was, "If someone starts something, be sure you finish it." And in addition to teaching karate, he also worked as a bouncer in a bar in order to, as he put it, "test" himself in the spontaneous demands of that position.

But such an interpretation of the man would ignore his deeper dimensions. Although he broke boards and bricks— or had them broken on him—his attitude regarding such displays seemed appropriately humble. My impression was that he staged these demonstrations primarily to test his own mental-physical focus and abilities, and also to instruct and inspire his students. He was a leader who led, not one who pushed from the sidelines; his instruction was active, and he fully executed the kicks, punches, and conditioning exercises he put the class through. He certainly possessed and exuded ample self-confidence, but he was never arrogant or haughty. Even his work as a bouncer he did with the spirit of the warrior, putting himself on the line to hone his techniques. That he did not revel in the violence of his job was apparent in the few anecdotes he would relate to those of us who stayed on to talk after class: rather than boasting of his exploits, he tended to recount incidents that were challenges to him, such as the time a bar patron of enormous proportions, with too much to drink, became abusive and dangerous and had to be escorted out. Sensei could only express his amazement at how one of his full-powered front kicks delivered to the man's mid-section barely even slowed his raging charge.

If under Arthur's instruction we were learning certain technical fundamentals, cultivating our perseverance under the challenge of hard training, and building a strong camaraderie, in Sensei's class we learned formal discipline, the complementary nature of hard and soft (in body, motion, and even psycho-emotional attitude), and increased application of technique. The styles of the two classes were different, but the actual basic techniques similar enough to allow cross-training with minimal confusion. Going beyond the actual karate training through weight-lifting, gymnastics-calisthenics, running, and speed bag work as much as time allowed, our physical, martial-oriented prowess was growing.

By our second year of training we arrived at the stage when the naive emptiness of the beginner's mind becomes clouded by too many unfamiliar and unperfected techniques, a fact we were reminded of each time we sparred. This was a particularly poignant knowledge, especially when sparring with Sensei or with the younger but equally large and impressive assistant who occasionally accompanied him. Our weapons were limited, and our ability to control *ma-ai* (Japanese for the combative distance separating opponents) by "closing the gap" to attack, or darting backwards or sideways in defense or to counterattack, was still virtually nonexistent. Worse yet for us, Sensei's style permitted takedowns in sparring, so we had to be wary of grabs and sweeps, particularly since our novice breakfalls barely protected us from the wooden gym floor on which we sparred.

Even hobbled by our confusion, lack of experience, and technical limitations, there were surprises, such as occurred during my very first sparring session with Sensei. He was awesome, intimidating, and I had nothing but the greatest respect for and fear of his abilities. Yet while painfully aware of my technical inadequacies by comparison, I was also too proud or stubborn to be bested in what I would have considered a humiliating fashion. Little of that first bout was memorable, but one exchange remains in my mind. While executing a feeble attack, I foolishly came within Sensei's grappling range: grabbing my uniform at the shoulder, he pulled me to him, setting up a sweeping throw. Just at that instant my body exploded into unplanned and untrained action, doubtless inspired by sheer unthinking desperation. The captured arm twisted abruptly up and over his trapping arm in one direction while my torso wrenched itself in another, and with a forceful jerk I was free!

As Joe Hyams (and Bruce Lee in Hyams' book *Zen in the Martial Arts)* would describe this, "it" had happened: I had acted without conscious awareness. In a state of mind devoid of conscious thought (called *mushin no shin* in Japanese, the "mind of no-mind"), something in me had erupted into spontaneous and effective action. When Eugen Herrigel finally allows his *kyudo* arrow to loose itself after years of frustrating practice, his Zen archery master does not fail to notice and stops the practice in order to bow in recognition of the event. Similarly, Sensei congratulated me at that moment on my excellent escape, which he knew was not based on some technical mastery.

This was an example in action of the untrained emptiness of the beginner's mind working like the master's mind. The advantage of the master's stage of development over the novice's revolves precisely around such occurrences: even if "it" can happen for the beginner, it comes almost as a surprise or shock. For the master, though he or she may intellectually be as ignorant as the beginner as to how "it" actually occurs, "it" occurs more readily, the result of years of repetitive practice and heightened awareness and sensitivity, brought to fruition in the imperturbable mindless mind.

The mastery of this no-minded state of action was the carrot attracting me, leading me onward along the martial way to self-mastery. But there was also a stick involved, something threatening and pushing me, urging me onwards in my martial development. Both Sensei and his assistant were impressive, intimidating adversaries. (After one sparring session with the assistant, for example, my shins were so bruised from the battering blocks of his Louisville Slugger forearms that the next day I could barely walk.) The knowledge that there were individuals of such ability, and that I was not one of them, threatened me. I felt that although I could account well for myself if someone of their caliber but of lesser moral development were to attack me, I was hardly confident of overcoming such a skilled and powerful foe. It was this threat, coupled with the deep satisfaction I felt through my training, that inspired me to fully embrace the warrior's Way.

INTEGRATION

For two years I trained in Sikaran and the modified Goju style, supplementing this training with other exercises. I had earnestly embraced the martial Way, and determinedly sought the mastery of technique and self it offers, although my conceptualization of exactly what that was remained poorly formulated. These were good years, strong and solid, a foundation upon which to build new and sturdy structures. While this might make it sound like I did little else other than engage in physical training in my last two college years, in fact, not bound by the rigid daily schedules of a sports team, I was able to craft most of my workouts and formal sessions around my class and study schedule. It is common to hear of the complementarity of physical training and scholastic endeavor; Sensei himself made sure to point out to us how important it was for us as full-time students to engage in regular athletic activity, to strengthen our bodies as we strengthened our minds. But actually, for the serious student in a comprehensive martial arts program, training and development encompass the total being: mental concentration as well as physical focus; heightened awareness and sterner self-discipline; improved control of our actions, thoughts, and emotions.

Academics at Colgate were of primary importance, but with all of my evident interest in the martial systems of East Asia, it is ironic that my formal major at Colgate had virtually nothing to do with the martial arts. Although I read Taoist, Zen, and martial arts tomes whenever I could, I felt my academic urgings in other directions. I worked with a committee of professors to design my own, topical concentration, generically labeled "Prehistory." In it were combined geology and archaeology, art history of the Old World and New, and archaeoastronomy and anthropology of native societies and cultures, particularly of the Americas.

The core of my study was most influenced by an extremely energetic and charismatic professor of astronomy, Anthony F. Aveni, whose primary study is on ancient systems of astronomy and calendar, how these are manifest in the alignments and orientations of the ruins of people who had once lived and thrived, and how all of this was integrated in the culture at large. Working with him, I had reconfirmed for myself the conviction, founded on my father's example, that the mastery achievable through martial training was also accessible to those who knew virtually nothing of the martial way. Having embraced his own Way, that of the scholar-teacher, Aveni exemplified the lessons to be learned from any Way to mastery.

The martial arts became an integral contribution to my undergraduate achievements. My growing knowledge of self and improving physical abilities strengthened my confidence, allowing the earlier me, a virtual stay-at-home, to venture forth into new and exotic lands. New powers of concentration and focus, new energies, new awareness were all developing as part of my college growth experience. On the actual day of graduation there was no category for recognition of my involvement in the martial arts or their contribution to my performance while at Colgate. No longer being on an official intercollegiate team, I was not eligible for scholar-athlete recognition. But I knew the part my training had played. And when at last it was my turn to stride upon the stage and receive my Bachelor of Arts diploma, what others learned was that I had earned High Honors in my major, graduated *magna cum laude,* and a selected member of the prestigious honor society of Phi Beta Kappa.

Although I had not known when I entered Colgate what I would do afterward, at graduation I knew where I would go next. I was bound for graduate studies in anthropology. And taking responsibility for the continuity of the Way I had embraced, I was just as determined to be bound for a new and even more significant involvement with the martial arts.

EMBRACING YOUR WAY

As described by Sato in the opening quote of this chapter, engaging in a "serious undertaking" seems to be the crucial, necessary condition for traveling the Way to mastery. Here it is you, the traveler, who decides how seriously you engage yourself in any undertaking, how fully you embrace your Way.

How can you choose your particular path? If possible, select an endeavor that interests and motivates you, one in which you can put your energies and creative talent. Musashi writes of the necessity of "long-term devotion" to pursuing the Way. Mastery will only come with consistent and persistent long-term effort, and so your chosen way should be an activity that you find interesting, challenging, or stimulating, one which you can embrace wholeheartedly.

Preferably it should be activity which is detached from an emphasis on making money. Although your "serious undertaking" might result in an income, making money as a primary goal can easily cause you to stray from the original objective of self-development leading toward mastery. It would be like trying to hit a target, in a game of darts or a round of archery, while your attention is diverted elsewhere. At the same time, be careful to not overindulge in the seriousness of the undertaking. Being "serious" should be taken to mean that too much attention on the trite and frivolous would be counter-productive; it should not bar humor or other light sentiments. There is dignity in the Way, but it must grow to be natural, spontaneous.

The concept of mastery is admittedly indefinite, and since any Way worth traveling is going to challenge your abilities and commitment, "mastery" in any form may seem illusory, a chimera. And since traveling the Way is essentially an endless journey, your objective of mastery can seem inaccessibly distant or itself become clouded in confusion. To help yourself,

set more immediate, realizable goals. This is part of the ratio-
nale behind the colored belts or ranking levels in the martial
arts, and is the norm for virtually all systems of education that
recognize successive levels of competence, such as grades in
school. Stages of development are also marked in artistic
endeavors, and are noticeable and expressed in improved control over your chosen medium. Setting short-term, realizable
goals can help you gain a sense of your progress, which in turn
will help renew hope and keep you motivated. Also, try to
maintain the freshness of the "beginner's mind" throughout
your serious endeavor. As martial artist Hidy Ochiai in his book
Living Karate explains:

> In Japanese, we often use the word *sho-shin* , literally
> translated as the "beginner's mind." *Sho-shin waseru
> bekarazu* ("Never forget the beginner's mind," or "Cherish
> the mind with which you started") is one of the guiding
> conceptions for every professional who strives for
> progress and ultimate perfection.

Above all, be wary of pretentious self-adulation. The more
we are convinced of our mastery, the more likely it is that we
still have far to go to truly attain it . . .

ACCEPT RESPONSIBILITY FOR YOUR ACTIONS

When a man decides to do something . . . he must take responsibility for what he does. No matter what he does, he must know first why he is doing it, and then he must proceed with his actions without having doubts or remorse about them.

—Carlos Castaneda, *Journey to Ixtlan*

I have always been interested in the languages, lifestyles, and beliefs of other people and cultures, and fascinated by the various ways in which they view the world and relate to it through myth and ritual. This, the enjoyable experience of fieldwork in Mesoamerica and the Andes, and the inspiring examples of professors Aveni and R. Tom Zuidema, led me to graduate studies in anthropology at the University of Illinois. But different world views and belief systems are also at the core of Asian martial arts, and I knew I had only gotten a vague glimpse of these through my training thus far.

FINDING A TRAINING HALL

As I embarked on my next phase of academic study, I also was determined to be more fully engaged in the martial Way, and one of my highest priorities upon settling into the Champaign-Urbana area was to find a viable martial arts school. I discussed this issue with both of my previous teachers before leaving Colgate, and they agreed that shopping around before enrolling was a good idea. It is common for martial arts schools to have a high attrition rate among new members, many of whom leave because of frustration and disenchantment with a system they really know nothing of, although perhaps have erroneous opinions about, before joining. Visiting the facility, talking with instructors and students, and if possible, observing a class, can help you decide if you would want to train in that specific style or place.

One system recommended to me was taekwondo, a Korean martial art then growing in popularity because of its speed and dynamic kicks. It seemed that the style was also often taught by Koreans, men who possibly had learned and lived, and therefore presumably would teach, Asian philosophy as part of their martial art. So, shortly after securing my belongings in the mildewed basement apartment of an old, and soon-to-be-condemned house, I armed myself with hope and an old phone directory and went in search of a martial arts academy. Unfortunately, when I arrived at the address of the only Korean academy listed, I found a dance studio rather than martial arts school. Assuming that Hyong's had closed down, I disappointedly moved on to the other ads.

In general my experiences at these schools fit a pattern. The highly ranked head instructor was not around, in fact usually only taught periodically at the "branch" school. The younger assistant currently in charge, although probably competent, seemed to have too little humility, too large a sense of his own importance, and was too concerned with financial arrangements. At one place the young man in faded black uniform and black belt immediately assumed a stance that was intended to be a relaxed or natural defensive position, the body angled with shoulder and hip forward to present less vulnerable targets and facilitate the use of the body's trained weapons. But rather than seeming natural, the stance that he assumed told me that I was considered a threat, hardly the peaceful and humble demeanor I was, perhaps unrealistically, expecting. Furthermore, the first words out of his mouth were about contract prices and methods of payment, and it took considerable self-control on my part to keep from bolting from the place as quickly as possible.

Other options to commercial studios included several university martial arts clubs. The Aikido Club was advertising a demonstration, so I took up my place in the small *dojo* among the few other curious spectators. There was a handful of students of both sexes with different colored belts, and a thin male instructor, immediately identifiable by his outfit, including a type of long and billowing skirt-like pants as opposed to everyone else's more typical training trousers. This was the first time I had ever seen anyone actually wearing the traditional Japanese *hakama,* which when worn properly, lends dignity and grace to its wearer.

Once the demonstration began, the instructor looked impressive as he deftly applied the subtle shifts, circularity, and redirecting of the attacker's momentum characteristic of aikido, and with which I was somewhat familiar through reading *Aikido and the Dynamic Sphere.* The club and its instructor offered much of what I was seeking: a multidimensional and apparently effective martial art with its physical training strongly anchored in philosophy. As I watched, however, I noticed a marked contrast between the instructor and the students: he was dynamic and competent, they seemed all too passive and hesitant. I was concerned about the intensity of the training, which I craved, and I had qualms about studying a style that made virtually no use of kicks or offensive hand strikes. Once the demonstration ended, I made my way to the instructor, complimenting him on his skill, and asking some questions about the club. I was dismayed to learn that he himself was only able to attend practice sessions infrequently, as he had recently moved far out of town. In his absence, a student brown belt would be leading class. I thanked him and left, knowing that the scales had been tipped against aikido, at least for now.

THE LOST SCHOOL FOUND

Although my preliminary search was fruitless, I was too optimistic in my devotion to the martial way to be easily discouraged. A more recent edition of the telephone directory listed the Korean Hyong's Martial Arts Academy at a new address. I found the brick and cinder-block building with its steel door propped open, and its dim interior cluttered with such odd furnishings as a cocktail bar and bar stools. Finding no one in the front room, I groped my way in the dimness toward a lit interior room from which I could hear noises.

"Hello, I'm Master Hyong. What can I do for you?"

I stopped there in the doorway to the plain, spacious room and took in the man who had addressed me in accented, but otherwise excellent English. He was of middle height and stocky, with short black hair and glasses, and wearing sweat pants and a T-shirt. Having never met either a "master" or a Korean before, I felt both awkward and deferential. I bowed, and tried to keep my introduction and explanation of my interest in martial arts to a minimum. Now aged twenty-two, I was a little put off by my own apparent insecurity or immaturity in this first meeting with an Oriental instructor, a feeling of bashfulness like being on a first date.

But Master Hyong's unassuming air put me at ease. Although a high-ranking black belt and impressive two-time silver medalist in the Korean national taekwondo championships, his manner was unpretentious, and his attitude toward me respectful. We talked about my martial arts experience and interests, and then about my plans and goals at the university. Having a master's degree that he had earned when he first arrived in America from Korea, and intermittently pursuing an advanced degree in psychology, Master Hyong was not only intelligent, but well aware of the time and work required to obtain a graduate degree. (Perhaps I was less aware than he of these requirements, or maybe I would not have been so keen on initiating both graduate studies and this new phase of martial training at the same time!)

It was only after this exchange that the question of signing up and payment arose. A bit sheepishly, I related to Master Hyong that although I was on a fellowship award that year—in fact, merit-based aid and part-time work had paid for virtually all of my undergraduate education—my financial situation put me just a little above poverty, hence my residence in the run-down apartment house basement. He then wondered whether I could use a hammer and other tools. I told him that growing up on a small farm had given me practice with a variety of tools, as well as a good deal of experience in home repairs and light construction. Pensive for a moment, Master Hyong then showed me around the old building. As it turned out, he had just bought it, and was in the slow, initial process of converting its two floors from their prior use as a private men's club to their intended use as a *dojang* (the Korean counterpart of the Japanese *dojo)*.

His plans included tearing down some internal walls and structures and totally redoing the available space, both upstairs and down, including a thorough cleaning and painting, and he obviously needed help. We struck a deal: I would come in and work a few hours each week in exchange for my lessons. And although his other, main academy was an hour away in Bloomington, his schedule had him teaching at least three times per week in Champaign, so I would be learning directly from the master instructor. I signed up on the spot. This too was a new experience, and even though we bypassed a formal time-length or belt-level contract (which most others signed; neither of my earlier teachers had required a contract), there was still a personal information sheet, liability waiver form, and even a survey which was part of research he was conducting on motivations for enrolling in martial arts schools.

I was now taking an important step in my continued martial training, accepting the responsibility for organizing my time, energy, and resources to pursue simultaneously martial training and intensive graduate study. But as Master Hyong and I bowed and exchanged leave-takings, I thought it all over. I had secured formal training in a traditional Asian martial art, under the direct instruction of an Oriental master instructor, and in exchange for not money but physical labor, which I enjoyed anyway, and which could even be considered an extended part of my training . . . I was so thrilled, my feet barely touched the pavement all the way home!

CLASSES BEGIN

That evening I was back at the *dojang* for my first lesson, not without a few butterflies fluttering in my stomach. What was immediately obvious was the need to buy a new uniform: my black, hand-dyed trousers were conspicuously out of place among the all-white *dobok* (Korean martial-arts uniform) of my classmates. I tried to make up for this by being as conformist as possible in everything else I did, and took up my position as the very last person in line, trying hard to observe and copy what the others were doing.

Master Hyong conducted his classes using both traditional and innovative methods. On the front wall of the *dojang* hung American and Korean flags, and we saluted these and bowed to the instructor at the beginning and end of class. Prior to ending our exercise there was a brief period of seated, meditative breath and mind control, and also at the beginning we all recited a ten-point student creed that exhorted us to honor such traditional values as respect, obedience, and loyalty to nation, family, teachers, and elders, and to develop ourselves in spirit, mind, and body. Most commands, and names for techniques, forms, and other incidentals were in Korean, and *dojang* etiquette was also based on Korean patterns. There was a printed set of rules to be observed, and class discipline was always tight, but not stifling.

Many of the principles, rules, and philosophy of Master Hyong's taekwondo system were based on values associated with the ancient *hwarang,* noble Korean youths trained in the warrior and cultural arts some thirteen centuries ago. Tracing their philosophical and moral beginnings to Buddhist teachings and mystical revelations, the *hwarang* code embraced a set of guiding principles and desirable virtues. Joo Bang Lee, Grandmaster of the contemporary style of Hwarangdo, lists the following rules in the first volume of his work *The Ancient Martial Art of Hwarang Do:*

> Loyalty to your country.
> Loyalty to your parents.
> Trust and brotherhood among friends.
> Courage never to retreat in the face of the enemy.
> Justice never to take a life without cause.

The desirable virtues referred to included: humanity, justice, courtesy, wisdom, trust, goodness, virtue, loyalty, and courage. Master Hyong seemed to draw deeply from this traditional well in shaping the character of his system.

The class was small when I began, permitting Master Hyong to give us personalized attention. He also made frequent use of senior students to teach the whole class or lead a specific group or part of the practice session. I learned that even to wear the white belt Master Hyong required everyone to pass a minimal test, including comprehension of a few simple Korean terms, the ability to assume several stances, and a basic technique or two. After some special drilling during the class, I was able to take and pass an informal test by the end of the first evening, thereby allowing me to wear the white belt I was already wearing, and the only belt I had ever worn in about two years of training. Not only was this a new beginning, but the recognition of progress on the long road to black belt and beyond. Even though I was still the lowliest beginner in the *dojang,* I probably felt the best.

THE DOJANG AS HOME

Although there were elements of Master Hyong's system I might have preferred be different, I was quite pleased to have found it. At first I needed to make adjustments in my techniques from the styles I had been practicing, while I was also learning new techniques. Fortunately, the timed format of each session allowed lower-ranking students to give attention to all of their basics, resulting in fairly rapid progress with diligent training. My initial progress was rapid, and included an early double promotion (skipping one rank). Further progress, however, did not come so easily. For one thing, my legs, especially the hamstrings, were tight, and resisted all of my efforts to stretch sufficiently. Consequently, since taekwondo emphasizes high kicks to the face and head, the backs of my legs were constantly sore. On some mornings even the short walk from my campus apartment to my academic department was sheer torture.

Choosing to simultaneously pursue intensive martial training and graduate study was easy, but sticking to my decision was something else. My academic fellowship required high scholastic performance, while my formal *dojang* commitment also required my full involvement. In fact, I met a graduate student or two who had given up their active martial training due to academic demands, and my own advisor specifically suggested that I drop the martial training to allow additional time for study. And to top it all off, in spite of my scholarship I was experiencing some financial difficulties, which other graduate students could overcome through part-time jobs. But having committed to both the academic and martial endeavors, I had no intention of dropping either. So it was that during my second year of graduate studies I made a change that brought me even more fully onto the way of martial training, but also had the practical side of reducing my living expenses.

Over the course of my first year, the other taekwondo students and I helped Master Hyong renovate his building. The ground floor eventually became a fairly spacious *dojang,* with toilet facilities, a reception space, and workout area, including a universal gym and other equipment, and a private office for Master Hyong. We redid the upstairs with plumbing for simple stall showers and space to change clothes and storage, and we also built in a plain cubicle of cell-like proportions. This was to become my room.

It was certainly humble, and hardly what most would consider adequate. But for me it was a dream come true, for by moving into the *dojang* I realized a cherished fantasy, inspired years earlier by the *Kung Fu* television show, of living the Shaolin monastic life. No matter that there were no senior monks or any other residents, no joint prayer or meditation sessions to attend or Zen koans to ponder. There *was* the guidance of Master Hyong as well as my inspirational readings, several days a week of group practice, the rigor of as challenging an intellectual endeavor—in the combined pursuit of an academic degree and martial enlightenment—as any monk ever underwent, and the tranquillity that living alone in a large building can induce.

Here were quarters and Spartan furnishings to suit any ascetic. My room held a desk and small bookshelf, a dresser and clothes rack, a small table, chair, and hot plate, and a simple mattress laid directly on the floor. Before the installation of showers, months after I moved in, I took sponge baths in the sink, and an occasional shower at the gym or a friend's place. Summer turned the upstairs into an inferno and normally found me atop my mattress on the ground floor, still sodden with sweat. In the winter, to save on heating bills in a building that leaked warm air like a sieve, the thermostat was turned to its lowest setting after the last practice session of the day. It was not long before I could see my breath, while all of the single-pane windows were solidly iced over. Although blankets kept me warm enough in bed, I began wearing a knit cap to sleep, and getting out of bed in the morning was sheer torture.

Knowing that this was likely my one shot at a temple-like experience, I tried to live it for all it was worth. As caretaker of the place, mine were the cleaning responsibilities, and with the image in mind of young Caine stoically cleaning the Shaolin temple, I scrubbed, swept, and in general maintained the place as if it were my own. I sweat profusely working out, so either a closet-full of *dobok*, or frequent launderings of the couple I owned was necessary. Since I possessed neither the closet nor the funds to fill it, and since there were no laundry facilities in the building, I bought a washboard and hand-scrubbed my uniform daily. Doing as much of my academic work as possible in the daytime and on weekends freed some evening time for more philosophical reading while in a stretch position and sipping from a mug of hot ginseng tea. Almost nightly I held candle-lit meditation sessions with the sweet smell of incense wafting in the background.

One of the biggest advantages of living in the *dojang* was access to round-the-clock training. There was the universal gym and other weight equipment at my disposal, a hanging heavy bag and plenty of space for solo practice. On days when no class was held I had the facilities completely to myself after a hard day of studies. And there were memorable midnight sessions, when perhaps due to restlessness, or being charged up from having seen a martial arts film, I would descend to the darkened *dojang* alone, in sweats or my original two-tone uniform, and pummel the heavy bag, train in forms, or otherwise fill the space with combinations of kicks, punches, and *kihap*, or focused "roars."

The strain of academic demands occasionally rose to frightening levels, complicated as well by my taekwondo schedule and my desire to live fully the martial Way I had embraced. There were times when after a tough day of classes the last thing I wanted was to return home to a host of people and practice sessions awaiting me. And there were certainly times when more normal living conditions and social life beckoned, a siren song of almost irresistible attraction. But no one had forced me into the life I was leading, and I accepted the responsibility for it. I could see in my own life and in most people around me how easy it was to rationalize our mistakes and deficiencies, and how many plausible excuses we could always come up with to explain our failings or difficulties. It became apparent to me that such easy outs could become terminal roadblocks to further progress along the Way. Those whom I considered the better models before me, such as Professors Aveni abd Zuiderma, or my martial arts teachers, while acknowledging limitations and difficulties, did not use them to escape from their work and responsibilities. And when teaching, these same individuals were less interested in any excuses for poor performance than they were in encouraging students to try their best. Through them I began to perceive that to try my best earnestly I needed a strong commitment to what I was doing, but that such commitment was made only more difficult if I were working on excuses for why I had fallen short.

ACCEPTING RESPONSIBILITY FOR YOUR ACTIONS

Ironically, accepting responsibility for my own actions allowed me to become more adventurous, to explore the diversions and peripheral areas of my academic study that challenged me emotionally, intellectually, physically, and spiritually, introducing me to a new world of developmental experiences. Accepting responsibility for our own actions forces and allows us to be more self-reliant, while simultaneously demanding acknowledgment of the many contributions to our lives from others. By not accepting responsibility for our own decisions, attitudes, and actions, we relegate primary importance to external factors in influencing our lives, thereby thickening the clouds of illusion in which we live. As I struggled with the challenges of unfamiliar cultures and activities, and strove to mitigate any limitations preventing me from achieving competence closer to my idealized models, I fought against the attraction of excuses. Martial training was critical in this process of accepting responsibility for my actions, since it demonstrated that through consistent practice I could and did improve, and that I was the active agent in this process.

The ultimate source of our inspiration, our direction, our persistence, and especially of our capacity for enlightenment is ourselves. This being so, we need to fully accept responsibility for our decisions and actions, and their consequences. This attitude corresponds with what D.T. Suzuki describes in *Zen and Japanese Culture* as the emphasis in Zen on self-reliance, and not "look[ing] backward once the course is decided upon." Relying too much on others, or blaming them for our failures and deficiencies, not only indicates a shallowness of character and a weakness of spirit, it is antithetical to progress on the Way. Rather, learn to rely on and be honest with yourself. Remind yourself of this by pondering the significance of the most revered object of a Shinto shrine—a mirror!

THREE

CONTROL THE BREATH

I remember how fascinated I was by the fact that even such a simple thing as breathing was subject to being relearned and mastered, as part of martial arts training. I had no awareness then that there would come a day when the controlled-breathing technique I had learned would save my life.

—Joe Hyams, *Zen in the Martial Arts*

Every day we wake up, walk about, attend to the chores of daily living and perhaps have some fun, then go back to sleep. While we are doing this, many bodily functions, such as those of the intestines, heart and glands, carry on involuntarily, controlled by our autonomic nervous system. And while these conscious and unconscious activities are taking place, one of the most important physical processes goes on, for the most part involuntarily and unconsciously, but still subject to conscious control: respiration. To understand how vital to our well-being the simple act of breathing is, we need only try to hold our breath for a minute or so.

Breathing supplies us with necessary oxygen and rids the body of waste products. But most of us probably do not breathe very efficiently or effectively. When perfomed properly, breathing does more than provide oxygen and waste removal, as important as these tasks may be. The act of breathing properly can massage and strengthen internal organs, and can help us either to calm down or get fired up, to relax or to energize. Properly controlled breathing can even save our lives under extreme conditions; in *Zen in the Martial Arts,* Joe Hyams recounts an incident in which his "Zen breathing techniques" helped him recover from a rare and often fatal viral disease.

While breathing may do all of this, developing and coordinating proper breathing for maximum effectiveness and efficiency is not easy. But it is of fundamental significance in martial training, and in other systems of physical and personal development as well.

BREATH AND MARTIAL TRAINING

My training with Master Hyong was a new experience along the martial Way: compared with the two previous, initial years, my involvement and activities were now more regular and formalized. A training session at Master Hyong's *dojang* was divided into timed components, with some differences depending on the day of the week. After brief meditation, warming up, and light stretching, we practiced both "formal" and "fighting" basics. The former included a variety of traditional stances—with self-descriptive names such as "front," "back," "cat," "horse"—and techniques performed from each. These traditional stances are mostly low, emphasizing hip and leg strength and aimed at linking the power of the lower and upper body. We were reminded constantly that proper form is crucial to the execution of technique. Specific drills included simple stationary or walking repetitions of techniques, such as upper blocks, reverse punches, and front kicks; *poomsae* (forms, the Korean equivalent of the Japanese *kata*), patterned defenses against multiple imaginary attackers; and paired up exchanges with designated attack and defense roles, usually in one- or three-step formats.

As a complement to these traditional skills, fighting basics are intended for modern sport sparring, for which taekwondo is deservedly famous (and has been seen by millions as a demonstration sport in several Olympiads). The fighting stance we learned contrasts with the deeper formal stances often seen; it is a "high" stance that puts little tension on the legs, but from which movement can be incredibly quick, and in virtually any direction. Similar to a boxer's stance, it is highly versatile. In it we practiced defensive and offensive hand techniques singly and in combinations; a plethora of kicking basics including straight, circular, and spinning varieties; jumping techniques; and endless combinations of all of these. In drills, partners paired up and exchanged individual techniques or combinations, and eventually sparred.

Master Hyong combined traditional and more modern elements of taekwondo into intensive sessions that included the use of a variety of equipment such as a heavy bag and handheld targets. Besides the many repetitions of basic techniques, combinations, sparring rounds, and formal exercises, each class session also closed with conditioning exercises, usually pushups and timed rope skipping. Frequently, Master Hyong would actively participate in class, and it was always highly motivational and inspirational to watch him perform basics or a *poomsae,* combinations or sparring. Like a placid lake at rest, Master Hyong seemed to be able to stand, sit, or walk with complete composure; and yet he was a dynamo in action, able to unleash tremendous energy and power at will. This was the most effective way for his students to see the possibilities of our training with him: powerful, quick, limber, and seemingly tireless, he himself was the embodiment of what one might accomplish.

As Master Hyong emphasized, one factor that helped him perform so masterfully was his ability to properly coordinate his breathing with his movements. This includes knowing precisely when to inhale and when to exhale. For example, a person lifting a heavy weight overhead can best coordinate the effort by powerfully exhaling with the pressing motion. Exhaling is also helpful when taking a blow to the body. Similarly, a kick or punch is most effectively delivered with a powerful exhaling of breath. This is clearly seen and heard in breaking demonstrations with the loud yells that accompany the break. This powerful exhalation that erupts as a shout ideally comes up from the belly; called *kihap* in Korean *(kiai* in Japanese), these roars indicate and help the coordination of our inner life energy or *ki.*

But Master Hyong meant much more by proper breathing than simply timing; he criticized the very *way* we breathed. He pointed out that most of us breathed too shallowly, utilizing only a small part of our complete breathing apparatus, and thereby cheating ourselves from full application and development of our abilities. Master Hyong called such breathing "chest" breathing, and contrasted it with breathing in the middle and lower belly. He referred to the latter as "abdominal" breathing, in which the muscles of the lower abdomen work the diaphragm to more fully utilize the lungs. This he identified as the healthiest and most natural form of breathing, and credited it with enhancing physical performance and endurance as well as stabilizing emotions and promoting the health of inner organs. If you are not familiar with this type of breathing or cannot imagine it, lay on your back on a flat surface and place a book over your navel, then try to raise and lower it with your belly as you breathe.

Master Hyong's philosophy and system of breathing is common in Asia, not only in martial arts, but in non-martial practices such as meditation and yoga. A Taoist-based abdominal breathing is also emphasized in tai ch'i ch'uan, another venerable Asian art, albeit one with strong martial underpinnings. However, deeper abdominal breathing is not exclusively an Asian practice, but utilized as well by wind instrumentalists and singers, especially in opera, in the West.

In Master Hyong's class we performed specific exercises to develop proper breathing. Both before and after our active training, we sat cross-legged with our eyes closed, attempting to breathe deeply from the abdomen. This is not easy for Westerners not trained in this activity; our bodies are commonly too stiff to permit the straighter hips and back needed to allow proper expansion and contraction of the diaphragm. Even in Japan, where sitting cross-legged on the floor is common, a cushion is used to raise the hips in seated meditation, or *zazen,* thereby straightening and relaxing the spine and stabilizing posture.

The more effective active exercises we did were those grouped under the Korean term *dan jun ho hop bop:* the *dan jun* (*tanden* in Japanese; *dan tien* in Chinese) is located just below the navel, and in traditional East Asian belief, is conceptualized as the seat or center of the body's strength and power. We generally performed these exercises in a "horse" stance, facing forward with feet spread beyond shoulder width, knees bent, and the torso balanced upright on this solid base. Taking a breath in while expanding our *dan jun,* we would push it out by contracting this same area and pushing our hands forward (alternatively hands could go up, down or to either side) at the same time, until all the air was forcefully expelled from the lungs. We would perform various repetitions and variations of this simple but helpful drill. We were also instructed about how to properly coordinate our breathing with our technical movements, when to exhale and inhale while performing *poomsae* or other basics.

It takes long and diligent practice to become able to coordinate breath and movement, and even longer and more diligent practice to be able to do so without the need to consciously control the process. However, although it may take years to master this style of breathing, the relevance of correct and properly coordinated breathing to both maximum proficiency and overall health is a critical lesson to be learned on the Way to mastery, and one that is directly applicable to daily life. While belly breathing may never save your life as dramatically as in the incident related by Joe Hyams, it can be helpful in many everyday circumstances. I have used belly breathing to help steady myself prior to tests and demonstrations, to ease pain, and to calm ruffled nerves or emotions. In fact, "breath control" is the second point, the "B," in a seminar I offer called the "ABCs of Self-Defense."

In taekwondo and other martial arts, abdominal breathing is fundamental to physical training. Martial training is intended to develop an entire host of physical abilities, including strength, flexibility, coordination, stamina, balance, speed, technical control, and timing, as well as fluid transition between muscular relaxation and tension. All of this development is enhanced by mastery of proper breathing. And while these physical achievements in themselves are important, Master Hyong made it clear to us that they are chiefly tools for overall personal development.

PHILOSOPHY WITH TRAINING

From the outset it was obvious that Master Hyong was concerned with more than our technical training or physical development. In this respect, he seems similar to other traditional teachers of taekwondo. Richard Chun expresses the holistic approach of this Korean martial system in his book *Tae Kwon Do: The Korean Martial Art:*

> Tae Kwon Do is an exact system of symmetrical body exercises designed for unarmed self-defense and counter attack . . . The significance of this definition, however, is only physical and superficial, for Tae Kwon Do means, more importantly, a state of mind. This, the control of one's mind, self-restraint, kindness, and humility must accompany physical grace.

At some point during every practice session, Master Hyong would stop and talk to us, sometimes a brief comment, at other times longer anecdotes, intending to help us tie the physical component of our training into other facets of our being, and our physical training in the *dojang* into other components of our lives. He would say, for example: "When you begin the study of martial arts, a punch is just a punch. But as you train you become aware of different kinds of punches and the various things that go into making a punch good and effective. Wondering which technique to use, how to turn your hand, or whether or not your body is in the right position can make the execution of a simple punch complicated and confusing, and so at this stage of training you are very conscious of your physical technique. Then, after years of hard training, a punch becomes again just a punch." Here he was emphasizing the significance of the clarity of the beginner's mind, of no-mind, and although I understood his point, it would be years before I would really feel or know it for myself. Yet hearing it from him helped us understand our frustration with individual technique and to see beyond it.

Stimulating our bodies and minds, Master Hyong led by example and verbal instruction. Two inspirational maxims he was fond of were: "Be here now," and "Let it happen." The first is a reminder to focus both physically and mentally on what you are presently doing: "While in the *dojang,* don't think of your job or school, your wife or boyfriend." Not as simple as it sounds, the ability to mentally focus is another stage on the Way to mastery, and is correlated in the martial arts with the ability to physically focus and project all of one's power in precise and instantaneous action (a topic dealt with in greater detail in the next chapter).

Master Hyong's second maxim can be a little confusing, especially for gung ho beginners planning to become the next Bruce Lee or Chuck Norris after only a few sessions. His point, as anyone who overtrains quickly discovers, is that trying too hard can be counter-productive. (The need to be patient and let things flow is its own lesson on the Way to mastery, and is further treated in Chapter 7). In illustrating this principle, Master Hyong often tells a classic Zen story (another version is related by Joe Hyams in his book cited above) about an eager student, who asks his teacher how long it will take him to become proficient in the martial system he was learning.

"About ten years," was the reply.

The student then wanted to know how long it would take if he really concentrated on his training. "About twenty years," the master responded.

Somewhat puzzled, the student asks again, wondering how long it would take if he put every moment of the day and all of his energies into mastering the system. "In that case, thirty years," was the laconic response.

Dumbfounded, the student inquired as to why, if he tried harder and harder, it would take longer and longer to achieve mastery.

His master's response: "With one eye fixed on your destination, you have but one left to see the Way."

Another influential anecdote of Master Hyong was about a Korean monk, who in seeking greater understanding, began the long trek to study directly under a famous Chinese Ch'an (in Japanese, Zen) Buddhist master. On his way through the mountains the monk became lost, and wandered about over the difficult terrain until he had no food or water. Then, when he was at the very limits of his physical endurance, he stumbled into a cave at night. While lying exhausted on the ground, his hand felt something round and bowl-like. In the darkness he drank from it, and it became for him a veritable elixir of life, the sweetest drink that had ever passed his lips. He slept refreshed and at peace that night, and in the morning cast about him for the sacred vessel. To his surprise all he could find near him were some old bones and the top of a cranium. On closer inspection, he realized that it was from this very skull, encrusted with mold and dirt, that he had sipped. Fetid water that would have been repugnant to him at any other time had tasted sweeter than the freshest dew in his dehydrated state the night before. Instantly enlightened, he returned homeward, no longer needing the distant Ch'an master, newly aware that the key to life and Zen is your state of mind. This story was especially poignant for me: I too thirsted for that sweet, fetid liquid of the Korean monk's enlightenment, trying to forge a unity of mind, body, and spirit, seeking to know and to gradually master more of myself and the martial Way I trod.

These philosophical messages were among the most valuable lessons of training under Master Hyong. They made connections between the *dojang* and the everyday world, between physical training and our related spiritual and mental capacities, between traditional values and the modern world. They were music with which my own inner being danced in harmony.

CONTROL YOUR BREATHING

Breathing properly, from the center of your being, is one of the most fundamental and critical practices of a healthy life, and is an invaluable aid in achieving mastery of your practice and your self. Emphasized in all Asian martial and artistic traditions, proper breathing is essential for coordinating the whole of your being, which is comprised of what many identify as physical, mental, and spiritual components. In mastery, these become one.

Abdominal breathing can calm you or steel you for action; it can be a source of tranquillity or a font of empowering energy. The natural practice of infants, abdominal breathing is healthier than the shallower chest breathing of most adults. Its deeper and fuller breaths cleanse and stimulate the total pulmonary system, which consequently helps the lungs stay healthier. It enhances the exchange of fuel and waste that are the very objective of the breathing process. Abdominal breathing helps stabilize and coordinate movement, and has a direct, calming effect on the brain and emotions. Finally, it stimulates the intestines and other internal organs, and contributes directly, in traditional East Asian thought, to the development of your *ki,* the vital energy or life force.

To practice proper abdominal breathing, you should sit comfortably. In Asian systems, the cross-legged lotus or buttocks-on-heels *seiza* positions are preferred, although popular systems of meditation allow seated or even prostrate positions. The main consideration is to be able to maintain comfortably a stable posture, with an erect spinal column from hips to head. This allows for the natural curvature of the spine, which also places some physical emphasis on the abdomen. Once assumed, this posture facilitates abdominal breathing, while also enhancing the natural flow of energy along the body's major nerveways, or the "meridians" in Eastern systems, which are considered the pathways of *ki.*

For improved breath control, you should inhale through your nose and exhale through the mouth. Controlling or reducing your conscious thought processes should be practiced simultaneously, initially by counting the duration of your breaths (1-2-3-4 while breathing in, and repeating while breathing out), or by counting the breaths themselves, for example, as you exhale. You can count to ten and start over, or continue counting as high as you wish to go. Eventually, the practiced calming of breath and thought processes while in this formal posture will be applicable as well while moving, and thereby facilitate progress along your Way, or lead you naturally to Eastern or Zen meditation, with its objective of stilling all conscious thought.

There are many systems of breathing technique, but the main point is to return to deeper, fuller breathing as a natural act. This type of breathing should be implemented as consistently as possible in your training, whatever your chosen activity, as well as in your daily life. An excellent time to practice and apply such breathing is while walking from one place to another, when taking a long ride, or while otherwise physically idle, such as while taking in a movie, concert, or play. Eventually, abdominal breathing can become your habitual form of respiration, enhancing your physical and emotional stability, stamina, and health, and empowering you along the Way.

FOUR

FOCUS

"Focus" in karate refers to the concentration of all the energy of the body in an instant on a specific target. This involves not only concentration of physical strength but also . . . mental concentration . . . Since successful karate depends entirely on effective concentration of body strength, focus is extremely important, and without it karate would become nothing more than a form of dancing.

—Hidetaka Nishiyama and Richard C. Brown, *Karate*

Master Hyong's system had a plethora of ranks, a whole rainbow of colored belts from white to yellow, orange, green, blue, purple, brown, red, and finally, black. Each belt depended upon the successful completion of specific requirements, including new techniques and even a written essay. Although I would have preferred a less ostentatious ranking system, most students seemed satisfied with it, accepting the new colored belt after each ranking test as the reward for their hard efforts, as a badge of progress, and as a symbol of their abilities.

One positive effect of a system of hierarchical rankings is that students learn to set, work toward, and accomplish specific goals, providing them a systematic method for achieving larger goals, such as the coveted black belt, by marking incremental progress. By the time a student reaches the black-belt level, he or she should realize that even this goal is but a humble step along a much greater Way, and that the very act of treading the Way sincerely and resolutely is itself part of the ultimate goal. Still, for some of us, particularly in the early phases of our training, the black belt beckons strongly, and we put everything we can into developing ourselves to be worthy of it.

FOCUS AND FIRST BOARD BREAK

When Musashi writes in his *Book of Five Rings* of "polishing the mind and attention," at least part of what he is referring to is the ability to focus mentally. We can compare the concept of mental focus with the clarity that an ordinary eyeglass lens provides its vision-impaired wearer; it makes the world more clearly visible. But mental focus can also be likened to the effect a magnifying glass can have upon sunlight; when manipulated properly, the magnifying lens can sharpen sunlight from a diffuse oval to a focused needle point of light, giving the focused rays the heat energy to ingnite a fire. It is one thing to be able to keep your thoughts concentrated on a certain topic or task, as Master Hyong's "Be here now" admonishes, and yet another to be able to pull all of your being together to needle-like sharpness. To accomplish this level of unified physical, mental, and spiritual focus at one point in space-time, and to do so at will, is one of the characteristics of mastery. In using the term "focus," its dual properties of clarity and power must be kept in mind.

Martial arts training is an excellent method for improving mental concentration and focus. Partly this is so because of the mental effort required to learn adequately the requisite techniques that allow one to progress in any system. As such, the martial arts are comparable to virtually any field of learning, whether in a formal school setting or outside it; naturally and inevitably, setting ourselves the task of learning something new will improve our ability to think, lengthen our attention span, and tighten our concentration. The degree to which this happens depends on our desire to learn, which sustains our efforts, as well as the quality of the teacher, the type of material being learned, and the overall learning context, including our innate abilities.

What makes the martial arts particularly effective in improving our ability to focus is the nature of the material being learned. It is simply not possible to study a martial system successfully without paying attention to the action at hand. A student in any school who spends time daydreaming will miss information and naturally perform poorly and progress slowly. But while a student in an academic classroom may find it possible to slip by with a poor attention span and fuzzy focus, this is impossible in a good martial arts program.

Why? Imagine yourself in a martial arts class such as taekwondo, in which kicks and punches are emphasized. Perhaps in individual training you can be inattentive or half asleep, although the physical activity itself should help you to stay more mentally alert. However, optimal training of kicks and punches also requires work with a partner, whether in controlled drills or more spontaneous free-sparring. Especially during the latter, a moment's lapse of attention or concentration—perhaps you suddenly remember the open car window as it starts to rain outside, or an upcoming test, or a hot date on Saturday night—and your partner's kick gets through your sagging defense into your ribs, a painful reminder of where your mind should be!

A similar scenario can be imagined in a class where joint locks or throwing techniques are practiced, such as in judo. Your thoughts wander, and suddenly the ceiling is spinning overhead, you gasp for the wind that has been knocked out of you, and hope that the joint that is just beginning to ache will function normally when you get up. Worse yet is the potential for hurting a partner by inattentively kicking or punching, locking up a joint or throwing. Here the lack of concentration and awareness of what you are doing can easily result in a painful injury.

Besides partner drills, most martial systems have other ways to test and challenge our focusing ability. One of the most fundamental tests is breaking techniques (or, in bladed Japanese weapons styles, *tameshigiri*, "test cutting") applied to a variety of materials. The smashing and shattering of boards, bricks, tiles, or mountains of ice blocks is among the most spectacular of martial arts events, and rare is the public martial performance that does not include it. But although many have seen such a demonstration, breaking is perhaps the most misunderstood practice of the martial arts. On seeing a large stack of building materials demolished with one blow of the hand (or foot, elbow, or head) we are appropriately impressed. But we may also wonder whether or not the materials had been specially prepared in some way beforehand to facilitate the amazing feat, or question the character and intent of the martial artist, who may seem simply to be showing off by performing it. In fact, after performing breaking techniques during one demonstration, I was approached by a spectator who wanted to know why I "got off" on showing that overtly "violent and macho stuff."

Reputable martial artists are, in fact, breaking the real thing in such demonstrations, although care is taken to ensure that wood and cinder slabs are dry, since such materials become denser or more flexible when damp, making them more difficult to break cleanly. To determine the character or intent of the martial artist doing the break is not so easy. Breaking or test-cutting is designed to challenge to the utmost our ability to focus and project power. Although breaking a one-inch pine board can be accomplished by the average adult with minimal training, other materials can supply an appropriate challenge to the technical ability and focus of anyone at any level. Wildly flamboyant breaking or cutting spectacles would seem to call into question the performer's humility, which ranks among the highest ideals of traditional East Asian martial systems. But since each break is a test of the individual performer, only he or she can adequately determine the motivation behind the act. There are some for whom breaking seems to come easier than for others, but for all students there can be an appropriate level of challenge that requires them to muster their ultimate focus and technique. Through proper training, these abilities can be developed and improved, with applicability far beyond the training hall.

My first attempt to break a section of a one-inch thick pine board came as part of my test for the rank of yellow belt or ninth *gup* under Master Hyong. I knew I only needed to hit the board hard enough somewhere near its center to break it. But hitting a solid piece of wood hard enough to break it requires not only the ability to focus physical strength. It also depends upon mental focus, to coordinate the effort, and especially to keep the brain from being intimidated by a piece of construction material. Even with good physical technique, mental control can be difficult, especially during a test or demonstration, with not only fellow students, but judges and spectators watching and challenging our concentration.

When it came my turn to punch through the board, I stood before the board in a formal front stance, left foot forward and knee bent, right leg stretched behind. Two other students secured the board at its four corners. There were several other white belts attempting their break at the same time, and we were all to perform simultaneously on a counted command. Excited and a little nervous, I readied myself by checking my distance and running through the motion of snapping forth a "reverse" punch with my right hand, settling lower into my stance. I also consciously lowered control of my breathing into my abdominal area. As I did so, I could feel a flow of energy while at the same time a calming sensation, and I also experienced the real focus of mentally blocking out all extraneous sensations. For a moment I knew only the piece of wood before me, and I looked at it with something like tunnel vision, so that even the holders disappeared. For a moment there *was* nothing else, and even the distinction between myself and the board became blurred. It was at that moment, exactly on cue, that my right fist exploded forward, propelled by my entire body and a shattering *kihap,* and then sped back to its chambered place by my ribs.

As my conscious awareness of the room returned, I remember seeing two things simultaneously: the wide stares of the board holders, and the remains of the board still clenched in their outstretched hands. The board was missing several inches of its middle, which had flown between and past the holders, who were left holding only its top and bottom thirds. Somehow, my focused technique and the grain of the wood had combined to produce this unusual break, since a board most frequently will split neatly in two. Just how much of this can be ascribed to my focus is difficult to gauge, but I can say that I have rarely achieved a comparable state of mind-body-object oneness in the breaks I have attempted since that initial board. It was a powerful experience, an example of focused action and a sensation that my mind-body has not forgotten.

EVERY DAY, EVERY MOMENT, FOCUS

By moving into the *dojang*, I had embraced my way in earnest, committing myself totally to training and living the martial way. I accepted the responsibility for this decision and the effect it had on the amount of time and energy I was able to devote to academics. As I trained, my breath became easier to coordinate with my movement, and my techniques improved. But staying focused continued to be a challenge.

On an average day I woke early, generally by six, and trained briefly, usually light stretching and forms, prior to having breakfast and leaving for school around eight. Virtually every evening I returned early to the *dojang*, where I immediately joined formal classes, or on nights when no classes met, undertook my own training, which included jogging and some work on the universal gym. Weekends offered the opportunity for different routines, starting with a Saturday morning class that had deeper stretching and more vigorous practice. The best and most efficient way to handle this tight and demanding schedule was to be able to give each task my full attention as I was doing it. But the ability to do so did not happen overnight.

As with many other learned techniques, focus can be practiced and improved every moment. Simply walking from point A to B for example, whether a five-minute stroll or a hike across town, is an excellent opportunity to cultivate focus. What are you aware of around you as you walk? How are you breathing? Where are others around you, how vulnerable are you? What message are you sending others about yourself, and how are you treating your mind-body as you move along? At first, to apply and practice this continuous focus is difficult and unnatural. It requires a deliberate transformation of the way we think about, perceive, and do things. But humans are creatures of habit (just think of the many things we do mindlessly each day, such as our getting-ready-for-bed or waking-up rituals), so the more we practice being more consciously focused, the easier it becomes to do so.

I cannot claim that while I was living in the *dojang* I developed the ability to always "Be here now," or that even today, after decades of practice, I have mastered this critical lesson of the martial Way. There are times when character faults and personal frailties lead us astray; when a selfish and overly indulgent ego reasserts itself; when the demands of schedules and responsibilities cloud over other sensibilities; or when we simply make mistakes. But returning to the training hall reminds me of the need to focus, and of who I am and am striving to be.

DOJANG CAMARADERIE

The martial arts can and should be practiced alone, but just as important is practicing with a group. There are obvious technical advantages of group training, such as the chance to develop and apply techniques and strategies against a challenging partner and the enhanced sense of control, timing, and distance that comes with this. Training partners can offer suggestions, supply valuable feedback, and be a source of motivation. And equally important is the social component of group training, through which we develop skills that allow for smooth interaction with different types of people, learn to control our comportment and manners, and share a human and emotional bond of similar interests and friendship. Ideally, training with others should also take us beyond our selfish egos, as we actively engage ourselves in learning from others and in turn helping others to improve.

With regard to social interaction in the training hall, the *dojang* is essentially a microcosm of the broader world outside. Our friendships and rivalries, shared challenges, confidences made and sometimes broken, successes and failures, are all the stuff of life. Of course, some personal and interpersonal mishaps occur, which we perhaps wish had not, but because they happen we know and understand ourselves better. And as we come to know ourselves better, we can better understand others, and work to accept their idiosyncrasies, faults, and differences. In this and other ways the martial training hall teaches, in its own modest way, the great lessons of life.

As Master Hyong's system became better known, it attracted a larger number of university students. At the same time, Master Hyong became interested in establishing a club specifically for these students. He felt that the intellectual development of university students paralleled and complemented what taekwondo had to offer, and he also felt attracted to the university constituency, among whom he sensed would be greater receptivity to his philosophical ideas and outlook.

We performed some demonstrations on campus, and with Master Hyong's encouragement I began to look into the procedures governing the formation of a new university club. Finally in September of 1981, my fourth year in Champaign, we officially founded the Illini Tae Kwon Do Club, with Master Hyong as head, and myself as president and chief instructor. Sessions were held two nights per week in one of the university's gymnasiums and, at least initially, Master Hyong was able to lead class once a week. Some university students who already trained at the downtown *dojang* were invaluable in helping to get our fledgling club started. Class times were late, from about eight to ten in the evening, and we would normally go to the club sessions together after class at the *dojang*.

Since there was some flexibility in running the club as I wished, within the general guidelines of Master Hyong's system, this experience was very rewarding. Although only in my sixth year of actual martial arts training, I had continued to read on the subject, and was teaching classes in my academic role in the anthropology department as well. In short, I had begun to form some specific ideas about what the martial arts were all about and in general how a class should be run, and was grateful for the opportunity to put my ideas into practice. And as all teachers know, teaching others is a great way to learn.

Club sessions were also rewarding, in spite of the additional pressure they put on my already overbooked schedule, because of some underlying bonds we all shared as students at the U of I, and because of the relatively high energy levels we generated. In the early days the club size was modest. But when we all performed the synchronized, traditional movements, our combined *kihap* would shake the rafters, filling all of us with a sort of positive electrical charge and energizing us all the more. In fact, one of the more difficult problems with these late club sessions was being able to "come down" from them enough to be able to get to sleep.

It was also in the late summer of 1981, just before my fourth year in Champaign began, that another change took place. This was the arrival in Champaign of Master Hyong's younger brother, Namsoo Hyong. We made new alterations to the second floor of the *dojang,* and suddenly I had a roommate.

At twenty-six, Namsoo was one year my senior, and a fourth-degree black belt holder in taekwondo. Shorter and slighter than his older brother, Namsoo had been a regional champion in Korean tournaments, and was athletic, flexible, and quick, with muscular legs and punishing kicks. He brought with him the latest in competition-style techniques and combinations, and immediately began helping his brother at his various branch academies. Since Namsoo's English was not as fluent as Master Hyong's, this was a challenge for both him and the students in his classes, but being younger than his brother and generally of a jovial disposition, he was easy to approach and well received by Master Hyong's students.

We respectfully addressed him in class as Sabeom-nim, a term of deference to his rank and teaching status. However, since I was also to be living with him, we needed some other terms of address for each other in less formal settings. Since the use of proper names is not culturally appropriate in such contexts in Korea, we settled on the kinship terms Hyong-nim, "Older Brother," and Ah-woo, "Younger Brother." Although we did not understand each other very well, and although there was a bit of the rivalry between us common among similar-aged siblings, the names did express the affection and mutual regard we felt for each other.

I admit to having mixed feelings prior to his arrival. On the one hand, I was excited to meet Master Hyong's brother, especially someone my own age and with whom I would be able to share a variety of experiences. On the other hand, my life at the *dojang,* in spite of the public nature of the building during business hours, was a very private one. While human companionship was attractive, I had also grown accustomed to my solitary abode. I was concerned how my schedule, which was intense and at times idiosyncratic, would fit with someone else's. Namsoo probably had similar doubts, while both of us were also going through maturing transformations in our personalities and outlooks on life. This all made for a difficult fit.

In spite of our busy schedules, however, we were able to spend some time training together, going to movies, and eating out. Our conversations ranged over many different topics, and we exchanged thoughts and opinions on virtually any subject. We sang, played, and worked out together, and the *dojang* vibrated with new life.

PREPARING FOR BLACK BELT

That fourth year of my residence in Champaign was a real maelstrom of activity: the start-up of the Illini Club, the arrival of Namsoo, and the culmination of my preparations for the black-belt test. Later in the school year I also took and passed my preliminary exams toward the doctoral degree. In Master Hyong's system at that time, the black belt, or *chodan,* test was a major undertaking, a milestone on the martial Way that, once passed, would qualify one to be truly called a martial artist. Besides a research paper, testing included repetition of all of the requirements of the many lower ranks, a grueling, multi-round sparring component, and the hand-breaking of two two-inch thick cinder slabs, without spacers. A failure in any of these sections would require a retest, some six months later.

The sparring component of the exam was certainly intimidating. At that time we were sparring frequently in the *dojang,* especially after Namsoo arrived, and it was as exhilarating as it was dangerous. In spite of protective equipment, my ribs were broken at least once, and everyone's shins and forearms were either black and blue and aching or eventually conditioned by frequent impact. And even though I tried to maintain a good level of aerobic conditioning, a stiff sparring session with a rotation between different sparring partners was always exhausting. To contemplate a multiple rounds of sparring with other black belts near the end of the long black-belt test was more than a little daunting.

But what challenged me the most were those four inches of gray concrete. They were set up horizontally at about knee-level, one atop the other, on two large, vertical cinder blocks. The preferred technique was a "hammer" fist, a balled-up fist with the outside (little-finger) edge as the striking surface. The object was to bring the hammer fist down and through the middle of the blocks. I had seen other black belts demonstrate the technique, but not always with success, so although I knew it could be done, there was also that little nagging doubt.

My first attempt at this break was actually at my test for what was called "provisional" black belt. This was the rank immediately preceding *chodan* itself, and served both as prepa-ration and probation for the actual black-belt rank. A friend of mine going up for the same rank was able to go through the blocks, although he severely bruised his hand doing so. When it was my turn, I faced the slabs and made some preliminary passes at it to properly position and prepare myself, then with a loud *kihap,* brought my clenched fist down onto the slabs with what I thought was all my might. However, this produced no visible impression on the slabs, which remained as unaf-fected by my blow as a wall is to the bug that crawls on it. Although my hand was sore, my pride demanded that I make another pass at it, with the predictable result that the immov-able object remained unmoved.

My failure disappointed and confused me. I was young, strong, and highly dedicated to the martial Way, and yet I had failed to break the blocks. What was more dumbfounding was that I had seen others complete the break who I knew to have less muscular strength. I had even taken first place in push-ups in an inter-*dojang* physical fitness competition, completing seventy-plus in one minute, with good form and on my knuckles. What had gone wrong?

Afterwards, Master Hyong critiqued my form, explaining its weak points. Because my body angles had been wrong on the attempt, I had not been able to deliver the full force of my blow onto the blocks. He also suggested I do more hand conditioning. Up to that time, hand conditioning in the *dojang* had received very little emphasis. There was one *dahlyeon bong,* or "striking board," in the training hall, made of split two-by-fours with wedges driven in the splits. By hitting the flat surface of the outer board, the spaces would allow the wood to compress with a loud clacking sound. We used it only sporadically, especially since it had been my impression that the success or failure in this sort of break depended particularly on the ability to focus mentally. And mental focus I thought I had adequately developed.

But once I suffered the defeat of the unbroken blocks, I realized that there were many components to a successful break, and specifically to mental focus. Physical preparation and good technique were essential, and were somehow interconnected with the mind. Once most of the tenderness left my bruised hand, I was determined to overcome whatever weaknesses had resulted in my failed break, and began doing serious hand conditioning, striking the *dahlyeon bong* first with the hammer fist, then eventually, as my hand toughened, with the opened outside or knife edge.

Due to the duration of the tests and the occasional long intervals between them, Master Hyong would allow the required breaking component to be attempted at a demonstration. Candidates in fact had three opportunities to complete the break, the last of these, if necessary, during the actual *chodan* test. I naturally wanted to get this particular event out of the way before then if at all possible. In early September of my fourth year of residence in Champaign we were going to do a demonstration to promote our new club, so I began to target that date for my breaking-technique test.

Unfortunately, the day before the demonstration, I injured my right hand during practice, not badly, but enough to make it sore to the touch. I debated with myself the advisability of trying the break, but this would be the last opportunity to attempt it prior to the October black-belt test, and since I felt my preparation had gone well, I decided to give it a try. Besides, having become more aware of the role of mental focus and mind-body unity for a successful break, I flattered myself by thinking that I would be able to overcome the minor distractions of a sore hand and the previously missed break.

The demonstration took place in the evening, and quite a number of students showed up to watch and perhaps join. Several of us from the downtown academy performed sets of basics and combinations, formal techniques and sparring, and then we ended the event with breaking, with my try at the blocks the last activity. While the blocks were being set up, Master Hyong prefaced my attempt with some comments about the significant interrelation of mind and body, and how martial arts training could benefit our academic performance, using me as part of his example. Whether he said this out of simple conviction, or as a way to put some extra pressure on me to succeed in the break attempt, or perhaps even to relieve pressure on me by showing his confidence in me, I felt my tension rise after his brief talk, and approached the blocks with some trepidation. In spite of myself, I remembered the seemingly impassable barrier the blocks were on my previous attempt, and feeling pain as I clenched my injured fist only added to my doubts. Taking a deep breath, I tried to clear my mind and replicate the mental state I had achieved for my first board break, years previously. I focused on the blocks, prepared my position, then struck—and again failed.

THE TEST

On October 10, 1981, barely a month after the Illini Club demonstration, we held a major test at the Champaign *dojang*.

As one of the higher-ranking students at the time, not only did I have the details of my test to think about and perform, but much of the organizational duties as well. Since students and parents from other *dojang* would be coming, and outside judges were invited, there was a lot to arrange and keep running smoothly—and all on the same day as my own demanding test for black belt!

It was a long day for me, organizing the comings and goings of candidates for the many different belt ranks, setting up for breaks or sparring, ushering different groups bowing in while others bowed out. We were all challenged by periods of warming up and performing, followed by waiting, when the muscles would cool off and stiffen up. In my turn I performed the required basics, all of my *poomsae,* or form sequences, and sparred several rounds, rotating among the other black-belt students. Perhaps it was my preparation, or the sensory over-load of the day, but even the intimidating sparring rounds came and went with a natural flow. As far as I knew, my test performance to that point had been good; even my high kicks in the forms had been relatively focused and smooth. Now I faced the last event of the day, those slabs of gray cinder.

In the month between the Illini demonstration and the test, both Master Hyong and his brother helped me prepare. Both seemed to recognize that there was some sticking point with me; perhaps at first I had relied too much on physical strength alone, and afterwards failure had shaken my confidence. Consequently, we worked on correct form in delivering the blow, in order to coordinate my power and get my energy to actually strike the block. And for a week before the test we tried a new training technique. Setting up two chairs, we laid a piece of paper across them, at about the height of the cinder slabs. They instructed me to hit the paper as if it were the blocks, and to penetrate through it to the floor. Time after time I drove my clenched fist through the paper, awkwardly at first since there was so little resistance. But because there was so little resistance I was able to concentrate more on my technique, coordinating the efforts of my mind and body. And by easily and consistently breaking through the paper barrier, there was the hope that I would break through the mental barrier that had formed following my previously unsuccessful block-breaking attempts, so I performed the exercise relentlessly. I also put more effort into coordinating abdominal breathing with this particular technique, using this to calm the mind, fuel the body, and to empower and coordinate my effort.

Finally, the time for breaking the blocks arrived. One student was to attempt the break before me. He approached the set-up, made his preparatory passes, then drove down his fist, but broke only an edge on one of the slabs. Once the broken slab was replaced by another, he was unable to go through both.

Following this less than inspirational lead came my turn, my last chance to succeed; failure would require complete retesting, many months later. Standing before the slabs, I took some breaths deep down into my belly. My mind went back to that very first board break and the sensation of that experience. Although I did not feel quite the same focus now as I had for my first board break, I was centered, the blocks were waiting, and the rest of the room ceased to matter. With a ferocious *kihap* I drove my hand downward and through the four inches of cinder slab. I had done it, while barely feeling the impact, and as I bowed to my teachers and judges and saw the smiles and heard the applause, I knew I had begun a new phase of my life and training.

BE FOCUSED

To embrace the Way requires commitment and dedication. This requires focus, the ability to concentrate on a given task at a specific moment in time and space. Such concentration allows us to marshal our energies and unify our selves.

Going through empty motions in practice, performing techniques mechanically, will not improve our form, let alone help us develop mastery. Rather, we must apply ourselves diligently to the endeavor, focusing on each move, every act. While this is particularly necessary at the early stages of training and learning, it is also applicable as we strive for any new knowledge, following Musashi's advice to delve deeper and deeper into our chosen path.

Concentration on a specific activity helps reduce the frequent chatter that goes on in our brains, chatter that is not only distracting, but that can lead to less than optimal psychological and emotional conditioning. Eventually, once repetitive focused training results in proficiency or technical mastery, such conscious concentration is no longer necessary; our ability to enter completely into our tasks, to lose our*selves* in them, will occur naturally. This is the stage at which we as doer can be said to have "become one" with the totality of ourselves and with what we are doing. The kyudo archer recognizes no distinctions between the self, the loosed arrow, or the target to which it speeds. The dancer *is* the dance; the hand of the Zen artist is one with the brush, paper, and painting, so that the result is one of exquisite and spontaneous beauty. Focus, in its ultimate development and made habitual through serious training, allows us to be tied inextricably with the objective, while allowing us the freedom that comes only with complete letting go.

FIVE

DEVELOP SELF-DISCIPLINE

Winning is not the basic goal behind martial arts training . . . that goal is sometimes called "conquering the self". . . The two basic elements that lead to and reflect that conquest are respect and discipline . . . By conquering ourselves, we learn these greater truths—that all people deserve respect and that discipline makes everything possible.

—Chuck Norris, *The Secret Power Within*

My successful black-belt test improved my confidence and indicated real progress along the Ways of both personal and martial development. I was able to apply the fruits of this success and see its contributions in other aspects of my life, particularly academics. After four years as a doctoral candidate I was ready for the grueling written and oral preliminary exams—the later, final examination is actually the defense of the written dissertation—designed to test candidates in all pertinent areas of their field of study.

This rite of passage, the preliminary exams, cleared me for the actual heart of the doctoral program: anthropological field research. My plan, supported by a Fulbright Commission Fellowship, was to live and work among the Bororo Indians of Mato Grosso, Brazil, identifying interrelations between concepts of space and time as manifest in such areas of their culture as astronomy, language, calendar, social organization, belief systems, and rituals. But I still required formal permission from the Brazilian governmental to pursue the research, and as I waited, my life changed dramatically.

While involved in doctoral and martial studies, my life was one of utter intensity. Rigorous academic demands, challenging martial requirements, and *dojang* asceticism patterned my life, and the constant demand for discipline and self-control was beginning to earn me a characterization that a friend of mine charitably labeled as "crusty." Somehow in spite of this, a young woman also in the U of I anthropology department and I began developing a mutual romantic interest.

Surabela was studying for a master's degree, and had just completed a year at Konan University in Japan. Her companionship not only helped me "lighten up," but her artistic background and sensitivity helped develop a softer and more creative side. When permission to do research in Brazil finally arrived, we were faced with some difficult decisions. I saw only one favorable option, so I proposed marriage. She accepted, and in character with her own courage and spirit, accepted as well the invitation to come with me into the hinterlands of Brazil. We were wed a month later on the autumnal equinox in a modest ceremony, and our mini-honeymoon was brief but ebullient. After it we made final arrangements and were soon boarding a southbound plane feeling both excited and a little apprehensive over what lay in store.

VILLAGE LIFE AND THE WAY OF ANTHROPOLOGY

Upon arrival in Brazil, we spent some time in São Paulo and Rio de Janeiro acclimating and making preparations, and then traveled to the interior. We spent the month of January visiting different Bororo communities, seeking to establish an actual field site. Although once populous and powerful, the Bororo in the early 1980s were limited to little more than a handful of ethnically recognizable communities, with a total population of less than a thousand.

After various travels and challenges we decided to spend the remainder of our actual research period in a village known as Garças (pronounced "gar-soss"), about twenty-five miles from the Salesian mission of Meruri in the state of Mato Grosso. We were driven to the village by jeep over the mud-thickened trails of the rainy season for what seemed like hours. Only with the hum of the mission vehicle drifting away on its return journey, and standing surrounded by Brazil's immense expanse of tropical savanna, did we feel the finality of our decision. We stood beneath a glowering sky, in the rain-soaked plaza of a ring of thatched houses, the center of curious attention and focused stares from its eighty or so inhabitants, and wondered what we were doing there.

The Bororo, themselves appearing to live on the edge of subsistence, had little to offer us in terms of material support, but they accepted us graciously enough, the nuisance of our presence perhaps compensated for by our entertainment value. Without electricity or plumbing or any of the amenities we normally take for granted, our life in the village was difficult and trying, but full of experiences that are generously described as character-building.

In the daytime, swarms of insects clouded our eyes, ears, noses, mouths, and any patch of exposed flesh, many of them biting or stinging, so that we were quickly covered with swellings and itching sores. Lacking our own transportation, we had limited our belongings to bare essentials, and we soon found ourselves suffering for lack of basic foodstuffs. During the rains there was plenty of accessible water, although all of it apparently the breeding ground for various parasites. In the dry season, almost all the local water dried up. A small spring and pool a couple of hundred yards from our hut served as watering hole, laundry, and bath, but over the months at least three snakes visited us there as my wife and I bathed.

Our temperate bodies attempted to acclimate to the rigors of tropical heat, months of pouring rain in the rainy season, and dry, dusty months in the dry season. Lack of properly nutritious food was a constant problem. (My wife often comments that my knees were larger than my thighs by the time we left the village.) There were the dangers of the forest, especially manifest on excursions such as the fishing jaunts I would make with the men, when we would leave the village before dawn and stay out until sunset, for much of the time wading and swimming through dark, mucky, and mysterious waters.

These waters had dogfish, which can sever a finger with one bite, stingrays (caught practically every trip, and with every man showing off scars of the painful stings of these creatures), and even minuscule schistosomes able to enter the body and infest internal organs. There were also debilitating sunstroke, serious dog bite, ax injuries, and other accidents or occasional near-tragedies.

But we stayed. We forged alliances, worked alongside our neighbors, began to learn their language, shared their hardships, sorrows and joys, and eventually sang and danced with the Bororo as adopted kin. Despite the challenges and pain, there were triumphs: the acceptance by most, the participation in elaborate ceremonies, the growing understanding of a previously alien environment and way of life, and our small contributions to the maintenance of village traditions. And we also wove deeper bonds between us, a newlywed couple depending on each other while struggling to survive and succeed in a strange land.

Our experiences were rich and varied. We once watched a tornado spiraling along a neighboring ridge, spewing forest debris like a breeze plays with leaves. In the "season of fire," as the dry season is called by the Bororo, we lay awake at night listening to the inferno engulfing nearby hillsides; during the day there was so much smoke that the sun was barely visible. We shared our tiny palm-thatched abode with an array of visiting fauna, including snakes, spiders, scorpions, and even marching ants that swarmed through the walls and sent us into the night nursing their painful bites and waiting for the seemingly endless column to pass. Of such stuff is the Way of anthropology, and it can be a true forge for the spirit.

In October of 1993 we left the village of Garças, carrying with us some basketry and notes and a multitude of bittersweet memories. In Brazilian cities afterward we convalesced and explored some of the Amazon and coastal Brazil. At the year's end we made our way back north, arriving for the holidays and the bracing shock of cold and snow.

FUSING THE MARTIAL AND ANTHROPOLOGICAL WAYS

While in the field I was able to practice martial techniques only sporadically, the lessons learned from my earlier training helped sustain me in this challenging experience. Of primary usefulness was the ability to self-discipline: no one was there to force me to meet the daily demands or overcome difficulties. To be productive, to get the most out of the field research, which, after all, was establishing the foundation for my professional career, I simply had to be disciplined; I had to reach beyond my normal mental and physical limitations. The previous years of toil, sweat, control, and discipline in the *dojang* were critical in allowing me to do this. The credit I accorded martial training has been expressed by others as well, and is eloquently summarized by taekwondo Master Hee Il Cho in his *Man of Contrasts:*

> I am a man of contrasts and have known the ugliest forms of life and experienced the beautiful; I have traveled much and learned from the many different customs and beliefs of many peoples; I know the pain of hunger that tears the humanity from a person but I also know the saturated feeling of fullness and plenty. . . I had one great assistant that never failed me but gave me strength, courage in the face of adversity, ambition and control of myself . . . that was Taekwon-Do.

Martial artists of long experience are unanimous in citing their martial training as fundamental to the quality and successes of their lives. What is of paramount importance is that these experts generally are not referring to the grappling, kicking, or punching skills. Rather, the message is that consistent and long-term training is credited with the development of self that enhances our ability to come to grips with the many challenges of life. As Chuck Norris expresses it in the opening quote to this chapter, with the discipline achieved through martial training virtually anything becomes possible.

During our anthropological field work, we lived daily in intense tropical heat, excesses of dryness or moisture, lacking sufficient water and food, exposed to dangers both large and microscopic, and among a community with a different language and customs from our own. We suffered accidents and injuries, fungal infections, skin lesions, intestinal parasites, and a variety of other maladies. And we struggled with the emotional and mental strains that such conditions, added to our stage and status in life, would naturally stimulate.

There are certainly people who successfully confront similar and worse conditions without the benefit of ever having stepped into a martial training hall; my wife's fortitude in the face of these difficulties is an excellent example. But this does not mitigate the physical and psychological support I personally felt from my martial training. During my field work in Brazil I began to understand that to be really worth the time, effort, and expense, a program in the martial arts, or in any Way of mastery, must be applicable in daily life. It must be something that you can carry with you and use, to improve your job performance, your interpersonal relations, your daily involvement, your total self. This "everyday-ness" of one's chosen Way is reiterated by Zen masters. D.T. Suzuki, expresses it this way in *Zen and Japanese Culture:*

> There is a famous saying given by one of the earlier masters of the T'ang dynasty, which declares that the Tao is no more than one's everyday-life experience. When the master was asked what he meant by this, he replied, "When you are hungry you eat, when you are thirsty you drink, when you meet a friend you greet him" . . . The object of Zen training consists in making us realize that Zen is our daily experience . . .

Throughout graduate school, my martial training helped me mature, complementing the more intellectual challenges of the academic Way while serving as the foundation from which to succeed in it, and allowing me to discover fundamental underlying principles of the quest for any path to mastery. I had embraced the martial way as a serious endeavor, accepting responsibility for, and any consequences of, this choice. I learned the importance of breath control and focused effort, and by being so far removed from disciplining overseers, having only my own will to direct me, I became fully aware of the tremendous import of *self*-discipline, truly the enabling force behind any traveler's progress along the Way. By having the opportunity to apply and understand the benefits of a quest for martial mastery in my professional work, as an anthropologist in an Indian village in Brazil, I drew nearer a stage of self-knowledge in which the clouds of a dimly-seeing and confused ego were beginning to clear.

DEVELOP SELF-DISCIPLINE

By self-discipline, I do not mean how you jump and run when told to by your teacher or martial arts instructor. *Self*-discipline is precisely that, a determination and power derived from within your self. Self-discipline is what directs you when there is no authority figure present. It must be properly developed and cultivated. Consistent and persistent training that requires you to regularly push yourself beyond your normal comfort limits will strengthen it; and once strengthened, self-discipline will in turn help move you to new limits of performance.

Although we all need the inspiration, motivation, and guidance of a good teacher, the self-discipline that allows us to push aside or break through all obstacles along the Way ultimately comes from within. To properly develop it, you must make self-discipline the focus of your attention. You can do this by setting incrementally more difficult tasks and challenges for yourself, and making sure that you accomplish or overcome them. This means not giving in to that inner voice of laziness or self-destructive whim. It can be helpful to imagine that someone you admire or respect is observing you: see what a difference this makes in your behavior. Such monitoring will eventually lead to positive habits, a natural concomitant to both self-discipline and self-mastery. To be self-disciplined lies at the core of mastery: without it, the goal of mastery is simply a wistful dream.

SIX

TRAIN HARD, SEEKING AESTHETIC REFINEMENT

Budo [the martial way] is not something that can be done in a day, or a year, or two. With training, there is never a point where you can stop and say "This is enough."

—Hanshi Sawada Hanae, quoted in *"The Meaning of Martial Arts Training"*

Surabela and I returned to the University of Illinois at Champaign-Urbana in January, 1984. We had been gone a year and a half, but somehow our experiences in Brazil put us more out of sync with American and graduate-student life than seemed reasonable. Known as "culture shock," such feelings of disorientation, a sense of being out of step with the surrounding cadence, are common when taking up foreign residence. However, they can be just as disturbing upon returning home.

For me, trying to use the new departmental photocopy machine just after arriving in town provided an instance of "reverse" culture shock. Our old machine had been a simple affair; after placing the paper so, you simply pressed a button and *voilá!*, a copy appeared. After living for about a year at the technological level of the Iron Age, however, being confronted by a monstrous new machine filled with various gizmos and menus of options, totally baffled my tentative efforts to produce the desired copy. I slunk away sheepishly, deciding to allow my personal cultural evolution to catch up with this new modernism.

There were challenges other than culture shock, such as our finances. As we finished our respective degrees, we survived through a combination of assistantships and odd jobs, temporary and part-time employment, and living within rather restricted means. A further concern was our health. Our time in the village, characterized by malnutrition and exposure to various parasitic and other infestations, had taken its toll. We were chronically fatigued, edgy, and with pains and malfunctions in our gastric systems. After a barrage of tests at the university-affiliated health facilities, we were treated for a variety of illnesses over the next several months.

But what demanded my immediate attention was what to do about returning to active and formal martial training.

TAEKWONDO REVISITED

Returning to the *dojang* after an eighteen-month absence was not easy. Of course, some of my technical competence and memory of forms had been compromised during the field work. But there was more facing me than merely refining some rusty techniques. I was shocked to find that the original building in which I had lived and trained, the monastic "temple" of my years pursuing the black belt, had been sold, and another, rented facility was the current *dojang*. And at the Illini club, only a few members remained of the group that had originally formed it. Worse, Master Hyong and his younger brother were experiencing very basic disagreements. With the abandonment of the old *dojang* of my earlier monklike life, it seemed an entire era had passed. New requirements, some different techniques, even a different belt-ranking system were now in place.

After some serious debate on the issue, Surabela and I decided that I should nevertheless re-enter the system, and that she would also begin training. We decided on emphasizing involvement with the university club. Besides identifying better with this group, there were only a couple of classes per week, and this would allow us the time to attend to other responsibilities, and to even cross-train in what we liked and needed in other physical activity.

Due to our relatively poor health, it was initially a struggle merely to keep up with the class. Surabela had never trained in a martial system before, and all the movements were for her unfamiliar and awkward. For me, some of the forms and techniques were rough, my body tighter, and in addition, there were whole new requirements for each rank—

which as a black belt I was expected to know—and an additional set of requirements for my next rank, that of *yidan,* or second-degree black belt.

As I struggled with the frustrations of relearning skills and requirements, and rebuilding endurance, flexibility, strength, and overall health, part of what inspired me was the fighting spirit and progress of my wife. Born with a congenitally deformed hip, Surabela has never liked admitting to limitations this condition places upon her. Although such a defect can lead to sharply reduced physical activities, Surabela has always developed and expressed herself athletically, and has even taught low-impact aerobics classes. Nevertheless, the type of stress taekwondo places on the hips through its many and varied kicking techniques, and its emphasis on speed and mobility was beginning to wear on her. In virtually constant pain, her gait deteriorated to a noticeable limp, for which she occasionally began to rely upon a cane for support, and this in spite of pain killers and anti-inflammatory medication which she took with increased frequency. She trained and suffered, and successfully kicked through a one-inch pine board, eventually earning the middle rank of blue belt.

What I learned from watching Surabela's struggle, empathetically feeling her pain and noting her stolid determination to continue, was a confirmation of what I had earlier noticed in the case of my father, who also struggled painfully for years to do what he could and felt he needed to do despite his deteriorating arterial and coronary conditions. The spirit my wife and father exhibit are clear examples to me of the warrior's spirit, an inner essence of life that burns fiercely, and is a font of strength upon which to draw. Ideally, training in the martial arts can help develop this inner strength, although it is my observation that this is not always achieved. And as the cases of my wife and father can illustrate, it is possible to have and develop this quality without formal martial training.

Active training remains the developing spirit's true forge, the fires of which sear away our impurities, temper us, and fashion out of our raw, innate nature a stronger and more refined self. To repeat the words shared in the introduction of the Japanese master puppeteer Yoshida Tomao, "From the day I started until today, every day has been training, discipline, learning. And it will be study and practice until the day I die."

My experience in the village had brought me into stark confrontation with myself, stripped to bare essentials. I was not satisfied with what I saw or learned of myself. From my response to the demands of village life I knew I still needed much work to improve and strengthen my spirit, as well as my physical and mental capacities. While I previously had understood intellectually the significance of physical training in developing the entire being, I now began to actualize that understanding. My training became more alive, more personal, more focused.

Hundreds of repetitions of basic kicks and punches were hammer blows on the red-hot, molten lump of my formative self. *Poomsae,* those patterns of combative response to multiple imaginary attackers, came alive as an imagined melee, with targeted blocks and counters, and the whole crafted with new dimensions of rhythm, timing, and explosive power. I even prepared and put up a *dahlyeon bong,* a Korean punching board, in the backyard of our rented apartment, transferring the forceful blows with which I struck it to the core of my inner being. Gradually my health was restored, and with it came a new vigor and vitality. After several months of this regimen, a significant moment occurred in sparring: in the midst of nonstop action I spontaneously responded to my partner's attack with a defensive, jumping back-kick, which I pulled just short of contact with his oncoming face and its startled eyes. I knew I had returned to where I had parted from the martial Way.

All of this more fully reiterated to me that consistent, frequent and rigorous training is fundamental to the warrior's way and ultimate mastery of self. Training in physical techniques is the most elementary component of the Way; it is the most basic and also the most necessary, and although elementary, there is no stage of a warrior's life or that of any seeker of mastery when it can be discarded, for it is the driving force of all other personal development. Men like Ueshiba Morihei and Funakoshi Gichin, who still actively trained in their eighties, understood and applied this fundamental principle.

On the other hand, hard training and sweat alone do not necessarily make one a master, of form, technique, or self. As Master Hyong was fond of saying, "It isn't just practice that makes perfect, it's correct practice." It is not enough to just do something over and over, but to do it striving for excellence, technical and aesthetic mastery. In true Ways of mastery, there is always this dimension of aesthetic richness. To master the Way is to become an artist in your heart and soul. The masterful musical chord, brush stroke, and even martial technique is not just technically correct, but also full of beauty and meaning, qualities that come from and are imparted by the master artist. Therefore, while training in the basics is the key to technical mastery, it is also the very process of practicing and honing physical skills, guided by a masterfully aesthetic model, that develops and refines the total being and the qualities associated with being truly human.

Training in the physical basics serves as the foundation of any martial or other art, and provides each traveler the essential skills to progress along his or her chosen Way. Struggling to achieve competency, proficiency, and ultimately full technical and aesthetic mastery of these basics is the true context in which real personal development occurs. Eventually, the punch, sword cut, brush stroke, or musical cord becomes effortless and richly expressive, a delight to the senses and soul of performer and spectator alike.

NEW LIFE

So we trained. How far through the upper ranks Surabela would be able to advance was questionable, considering that requirements included powerful breaks with dynamic jumping techniques very likely beyond her body's capacity to perform. We will never know, since it became expedient for Surabela to curtail her involvement with the system once we received the exciting news, almost a year after returning home, that she was carrying our child.

Like many parents-to-be, we were thrilled, awed, and humbled by the knowledge of this new life growing within. Thoughts of a larger family made us aware of new responsibilities, and the changes in our lives that would be required. Chiefly, the knowledge of fast-approaching parenthood highlighted for us the need for more economic security, and the completion of our academic work. Surabela's master's thesis, focusing on her successful apprenticeship in the process of palmworking among the Bororo, was progressing, but now the pressure was on to finish it. My doctoral dissertation was going more slowly, and required carefully organizing and analyzing my field data, writing and rewriting drafts, scrawling diagrams, and voluminous reading.

Rebecca Esther was born on a Saturday afternoon in early August, ten days ahead of schedule, the first hint of her general precocity. She quickly became the focus of much of our attention and energy. There is probably no adequate way to convey to those who have not parented, the joys, worries, thrills, and frustrations of this role, and no need to describe them for those who have. For me, the desire to be as actively involved as possible with the baby wrought havoc on my schedules. I remember one Saturday morning's upper-belt training session at the new *dojang,* after a series of sleep-deprived nights, watching the *dojang* walls spin around while I attempted to recover from too many sets of basic kicks and combinations. There were times it was necessary for me to miss formal classes due to responsibilities at home, and days when the only workout I could manage was a brief training session in the early morning or just before bed. But keeping our lives together and focused during this period also contributed to our personal growth.

DISSERTATION DEFENSE AND YIDAN ATTACK

Surabela successfully completed her work for the master's degree in anthropology prior to giving birth, but my doctoral work was taking much longer. The academic year of 1985–86, starting shortly after Rebecca's birth, sped by with me juggling my time between family, working out, dissertation writing, and teaching. Progress was made on all fronts, and our growing involvement as a family raising a new and increasingly sentient being continued to open up fresh windows of wonder for us. Nevertheless, although parenting was full of magic and rewards, it was also full of the annoyances and frustrations of illness, dirty diapers, colic, and disturbed sleep.

How does a parent attend to a sick and squalling infant with the calm of a master's mind? How can the demands of the everyday world be met calmly and with detachment, especially after successive nights of deprived of sleep? While it may be that living Zen is simply being what you are doing when you are doing it, as D.T. Suzuki is earlier quoted as advising, the fact that masters such as he often lived removed from life's more trying and mundane realities somewhat weakens the argument. One of the greatest karate masters, Funakoshi Gichin, was apparently able to realize the mind of mastery in his martial arts and daily life to a great extent. And yet, in the forward to his autobiography *Karate-Do: My Way of Life,* the president of Funakoshi's karate organization writes that for a man of Funakoshi's class, "the kitchen was forbidden territory . . . Nor did he ever bother to utter the names of such mundane articles as socks or toilet paper." Hearing of someone such as this being able to achieve the mind of mastery does not lessen the significance of his accomplishment, but leaves us with the question: How do we develop and apply mastery in our day-to-day mundane existence?

Probably some period of relative isolation from mundane demands is beneficial to any traveler's progress on the Way. But any worthwhile personal development should be applicable in daily life, and any life can be enhanced by the enrichment of characteristics cultivated along the Way. Still, attempting to achieve and apply mastery, especially outside of the training hall while beset with innumerable demands of the mundane world, can be a difficult and baffling enterprise.

While I have no secret solutions to this dilemma, the lessons of mastery as discussed here should help and sustain anyone in strenuous circumstances. They are principles fundamental to the mastery of art and self, and to the living of a life of beauty and worth. While cultivated in a training hall in active pursuit of the Way, they achieve their greatest relevance through application in daily life.

My daily life included the impending reality of my dissertation defense: the final doctoral exam. It was a grueling affair, with my committee's expectations very high. But my work was solid, and I passed. With some revisions and final filing, this milestone along the academic Way was finally in sight.

There was one more test for me before we left Champaign-Urbana, that of my *yidan,* or second-degree black belt, in taekwondo. It was now three years after our return from Brazil, and I proceeded through the demanding performance of a myriad of *poomsae,* basic techniques, sparring, and other drills as a somewhat different person from who I was at the *chodan,* the first-degree black belt test. Finally, I faced two boards held together: to break them, I had to jump up and over two crouching students, and rotating completely, execute what we called a 360-degree, jumping back-kick. With my *kihap* and the satisfying crack of the wood I became aware of a newly emerging self, a new integration of mind-body-spirit. I successfully passed my *yidan* test, and we began to prepare for the next phase of our lives.

TRAIN, SEEKING AESTHETIC REFINEMENT

There is no substitute in the process of mastering self for consistent and diligent training in the basics of your Way. Musashi's *Book of Five Rings* is filled with the exhortation to "practice ceaselessly." Only by emphasizing the basic skills or techniques can you achieve the artless art, the formless form of mastery. As will be further discussed in Chapter 9, whether these basics are kicks and punches, sword cuts, brush strokes, musical scales, or gardening chores, you eventually must be able to perform them well without conscious thought. As Yagyu Munenori explains in his treatise on the school of Yagyu Shinkage Ryu:

> As your training continues, the mind set to do well what is done will recede into the distance, and whatever you do, you will do without thinking, without intending, regardless of yourself . . . That is when you are not aware of yourself, and your arms and legs do whatever they are supposed to do without your mind contriving things—that is when you do right whatever you do ten out of ten times.

Thus, you are able to perform naturally, even responding without thought to attack, conjuring a response unconsciously, directly from your inner well of creativity. It is the same for all arts and ways. As Takuan expresses it in "Fudochi Shinmyo Roku:" "Training is the method of not stopping your mind in one place." Serious training in technique and form unfetters the mind, allowing it freedom to let go. Ultimately, you become one with what you are doing; intention becomes action.

While training is the main key to mastery of technique, the process of technical mastery is also the tool kit used to master yourself, the forge upon which you hammer out imperfections and weaknesses, while solidifying virtuous essence. These related processes require more than mere mechanical and dull repetition, however. They require your heart and soul, guided by a sense of beauty and correctness of technique and form that you observe in the patterns of your teacher and those who have traveled your Way before you. From those who have gone before we learn a model of aesthetically right technique and form. This aesthetic refinement of mastery lifts the Way above mere technical competence or mechanical proficiency. Aesthetic refinement enriches and humanizes the process of personal growth and mastery. It is an important part of the difference between the sword that coldly and efficiently takes life and the sword that gives, nurtures, and develops life. The heightening of aesthetic awareness and struggling for its refinement also helps to develop our proper conduct and expression, and thereby deepens our sensitivity as human beings.

SEVEN

BE PATIENT AND FLOW

Those who are patient in the trivial things in life and control themselves will one day have the same mastery in great and important things.

—Bong Soo Han, quoted in *Zen and the Martial Arts*

The more I attempted to learn and apply the physical and philosophical dimensions of Asian martial systems and the Way of mastery, the more I was drawn to actually experience them in their natural cultural context. Motivation was supplied as well by my studies in anthropology, which teaches that cultural components are integrated, in this case implying that whatever Asian martial arts are all about is in some fundamental way connected with other aspects of the cultures of their origin. The traditional martial systems of Asia were an integral part of their societies and their histories, and thus contributed greatly to the characters of the contemporary nations that developed from them. For Japan, Nitobe Inazo's text *Bushido: The Soul of Japan* is explicit on the significance of samurai training and ethos to the development of this nation that seems to have global significance out of all proportion to its modest size.

With this in mind, once my graduate responsibilities were concluded and with the happy coincidence of a job offer from a Japanese firm in Surabela's hands, we made a logical, and momentous, decision. We stored, sold, gave away, and threw out some of our possessions, packed and shipped the rest, and soon followed them to Japan. There we lived and worked for the next three years, learning about the land and its people, norms and standards, traditions and changes, and ourselves.

UNDERSTANDING JAPAN

While it may be that the brilliance of the Japanese economic miracle has dimmed of late, few can doubt the impressiveness of that nation's rise from defeat in World War II to its current position of economic importance. Japan is, for example, second only to the U.S. in annual GNP, and is touted as the world's leading donor nation in the area of foreign aid. These accomplishments are all the more impressive when we consider how little in the way of natural resources Japan possesses to facilitate this level of success.

Historically, the Japanese have developed as an energetic and disciplined people, whose social system and cultural norms emphasize tight-knit groups with a productive work ethic, and to which attention to obligation is paramount. Contributing factors in the development of these characteristics are Japan's natural setting, geography, and distribution of natural resources. It is a nation of mountainous islands in which the subsistence base for a developing civilization needed to be wrested from land circumscribed by ocean and steep slopes. Another contributing factor has been the destructive natural calamities such as earthquakes and typhoons, and their potential side effect, the *tsunami,* our misnomered "tidal" wave, which have periodically leveled communities, and from which survivors have repeatedly reconstructed their social and cultural, as well as physical structures.

What is cause and what is effect in the development of Japanese attributes is debatable, but an important shaping force in their development is a martial ethos that has pervaded Japanese civilization for centuries. For over 250 years during the Tokugawa era (1600–1868), the *bushi,* or samurai, Japan's warrior class, were essentially at the top of a caste-like social system. But long before this, at least from the twelfth century, when fighting between rival Taira and Minamoto clans resulted in military domination of a government until then administered by the nobility, Japan's military leaders wielded considerable social and political power, facilitated by their ability to control polity through force of arms.

Besides the discipline inherent in efficient and successful military organization, other Japanese characteristics are said to be associated with Japan's *bushi*. An outgrowth of the philosophical and religious precepts of Shinto, Taoism, Confucianism, and Buddhism, a code of conduct of the samurai evolved over time, as well as in different feudal domains. But the more or less comparable codes within which these warriors trained and developed has come to be known as *bushido*, the Way of the Warrior.

The earliest treatise on this subject written by a Japanese for a Western audience (in English) is *Bushido: the Soul of Japan* by Nitobe Inazo, who based his work, in his own words, on "what I was told and taught in my youthful days, when feudalism was still in force." In it, Nitobe lists the most salient attributes of *bushido* as righteousness, courage, benevolence, politeness, veracity, sincerity, honor, personal dignity, loyalty, duty, and self-control. These attributes reflect the "Five Constant Virtues" of Confucian tradition—benevolence, righteousness, propriety, wisdom, and trust—that Warner and Draeger list in *Japanese Swordsmanship*. As in the case of most ideals, there certainly exist deviations from and excesses in the application of these traits. But Nitobe's main point is that much of what is extolled as the character of Japan, indeed the nation's "soul," as indicated in the subtitle of his book, derives from the tenets of *bushido*.

Although Japan has changed significantly since Nitobe's era, his words are still worth heeding:

> He who would understand twentieth-century Japan must know something of its roots in the soil of the past. Even if now as invisible to the present generation in Nippon as to the alien, the philosophic student reads the results of today in the stored energies of ages gone.

I was curious to experience for myself this land of the samurai, to know what it had become, and to learn from what it still had to offer.

IN THE LAND OF THE SAMURAI

Surabela was hired by a firm providing instructional services in international communication, which would make use of her administrative, linguistic, and multi-cultural skills. Since the firm was a subsidiary of the enormous Sumitomo keiretsu, or "business family," we were able to move into subsidized company housing. This had the advantage of relieving us from the hassles of finding a place on our own, and of reducing our rent. Residence in company housing also came with a ready-made neighborhood; other Sumitomo employees and their families, a sort of work-based extended family.

Although in Japan you can see breathtaking natural beauty, as well as inspiring ages-old shrines and temples of hand-hewn timber, most Japanese (and foreign residents) live in urban settings surrounded by asphalt, glass, and concrete; bustling traffic of cars, commuter trains, bicycles, and swarms of pedestrians; and skyscrapers and sky-high prices. The area in which we lived, Koshien—a district of Nishinomiya which is about half-way between the larger centers of Osaka and Kobe—is typical of urbanized Japan, and famous as host to the biannual high school baseball national championships. It is a busy place, full of the inevitable noise, smog, and occasional congestion of the modern city. But it also has its charm, especially in its scattered pockets of traditional structures. There were small neighborhood Shinto shrines with their prominent *torii* (entry gate), Chinese-inspired architecture, and miniature, sculpted gardens. Streets were clean, tidy, and relatively crime-free. And, most importantly, there were the Japanese themselves, who place a high value on courtesy, and who helped us feel welcome, if not actually at home.

Our apartment, called in Japan a "2DK" (that is, two rooms, with a dining-kitchenette area), was a common type and tiny by American standards, at least for a family. Our living area was comprised of two six-*tatami* mat rooms *(tatami,* a rush used extensively for flooring mats, is affixed to frames which measure about three by six feet), a kitchen with barely room for a card-table, a short hall, toilet and bath rooms (separate and closet-sized), an entry alcove (the ubiquitous *genkan,* where shoes are removed before entering), and a narrow balcony. For storage, closets ran the length of each tatami room, in which the folded bedding *(futon)* is kept during the day, as well as all clothes and other personal belongings. The inconveniences of this apartment, its small size and lack of central heating, were somewhat compensated for by the tastefully decorated sliding doors *(fusuma)* dividing the internal spaces, and the paper window shutters *(shoji)* that illuminate with a pleasant, diffuse light, while nevertheless concealing the inside from the outside.

Fortunately, my wife had not only begun learning Japanese intensively during her previous stay in Japan, but had continued to take courses in it at the University of Illinois, and had become quite fluent. Unfortunately for me, except for a short cram course two weeks before our departure, I had never formally studied the language. Once Surabela began her full-time employment, I was left at home with our two-year-old daughter, with virtually no communication skills and playing househusband in a land where men are rarely seen at home during daytime hours. On most days, Rebecca and I would join the other company children and their mothers for play in a large sandbox and on park equipment, where Rebecca, with her dark hair and the advantage of the pre-pubescent brain for language acquisition, quickly became acculturated and functionally bilingual.

For me it was not easy, although I was able to complement my individual language study from books and audio tapes with daily application in real-life contexts. This resulted in fairly rapid progress in spoken Japanese, especially during the first six months of our stay. My motivation was high, and there were certainly an abundance of learning aids and practice opportunities available. But it was awkward being the only adult male among the daily groups of interacting children and mothers, and this limited the extent to which I felt comfortable practicing my rudimentary Japanese. Also, Japanese men and women use different modes of expression, which complicated the learning process given my situation.

We bought bicycles and an attached seat for Rebecca, so she and I were able to take rides for shopping or sightseeing, or jaunts to the seashore, not very distant, although access to it was restricted by a high sea wall. Even though these rides relieved some of the monotony and discomfort of my daily schedule, I knew that for the sake of Rebecca's socialization and normal development, she needed regular contact and play with other children, and so as often as not, we played near our apartment.

Besides studying the language and having the primary responsibilities for taking care of our apartment and daughter, I was seriously attempting to reshape my doctoral dissertation into book format. The irony of having been intensely involved in Asian martial arts while preparing a doctoral thesis on South America in the U.S., and then writing a book on Brazilian Indians while in Japan, was not lost on me. I don't doubt that my ability to totally immerse myself in any one specific project was affected by these diverse and competing interests, and perhaps this unnecessarily complicated my life. However, it seemed the only reasonable course of action, especially since all of my various interests seemed to demand expression. Besides, I was not sure then, nor am I any more certain now, that exclusive emphasis on one area of study is beneficial, or even desirable. This view underlies my staunch advocacy of the liberal arts education, which stresses a broad foundation of study in the humanities, arts, and social and natural sciences. Such a grounding not only ensures well-rounded development, but also allows for focused study in a way that should maximize the potential for cross-disciplinary connections. Making these bigger, interdisciplinary connections was part of what I hoped to achieve by my mix of interests and activities.

To make progress with such diverse interests depends obviously on an ability to focus, to concentrate on the matter at hand, especially since one may be changing the subject of one's attention dramatically in a relatively short period. It also requires patience, since the acquisition of knowledge, especially on disparate subjects simultaneously, is unlikely to come quickly or easily. (It bears repeating that both patience and the ability to focus are enhanced by serious martial training.) So I attended to my house-husbanding and parental duties; studied the language and the culture; and worked on my book, focusing on each in turn, and struggling with my impatience to know more, communicate better, and be more productive in my new environment. This was the everyday context of my entry into Japan. But my personal, primary reason for being in Japan was not forgotten: formal training in a traditional Japanese martial art. And thankfully, this opportunity was not long in coming.

HONTAI YOSHIN RYU JUJUTSU

Japan is known for its plethora of martial systems, including such a widespread modern sport as judo and the Okinawa-derived karate. Since I had no interest in competition, both judo and kendo held little attraction for me in terms of my training, and karate, although there are many varieties depending on the specific *ryu,* or school, was also less appealing to me due to its at least superficial similarity to taekwondo in emphasizing kicking and punching techniques. I was hoping to train in a style that could complement these techniques, one that emphasized joint locking and throwing in order to immobilize an attacker, and possibly some traditional weapons use. Being in Japan, I also sought something quintessentially Japanese.

Master Hyong, knowing my philosophical interests in the arts, had suggested perhaps the most obvious choice, aikido. Aikido was established as a new martial style during the middle decades of this century by Ueshiba Morihei, a gifted martial artist and devoutly religious man, who elaborated upon the base of his formal training in traditional styles of jujutsu, aiki-jujutsu, and kenjutsu to devise a system that he felt allowed a person to harmonize with universal energy. My earliest personal contact with aikido had been the club demonstration at the University of Illinois, and while the instructor had been impressive, I had doubts about my fit, at least at that time, with such a style, especially as it was practiced there. As it turned out, there simply were no aikido classes anywhere near or moderately convenient to our residence in Koshien, so involvement in that art was again stymied.

Another martial art that interested me was jujutsu (also jiu-jitsu and other spellings). Nitobe lists jujutsu as among the curriculum of *bushido* studies, and defines it as "an application of anatomical knowledge . . . to incapacitate one for action for the time being." One of the first Japanese instructors of jujutsu to teach in America, Kiyose Nakae, gives more substance to the definition in his 1958 instructional manual, *Jiu Jitsu Complete:* "*jiu means* 'gentle, pliable, virtuous, to submit' and *jitsu* means 'art or science.'" Its techniques were perceived by Westerners as so unlike fighting that they are labeled "tricks" in this relatively early English publication, and are said to "wipe out differences of size, weight, height and reach."

The potential problem in training true traditional jujutsu however, is its lack of accessibility. Several Japanese friends in the U.S. I had spoken to prior to leaving were convinced that jujutsu was no longer practiced in Japan, and that the more modern judo was the only existing form of this art. This sentiment is even expressed by the publisher in his original preface to Nakae's text: "Jiu Jitsu is no longer taught in Japan. It is no longer passed from generation to generation, as it had been for hundreds of years." I doubted that I could even find a jujutsu school, let alone one close enough for me to train in, and that would accept a foreigner into its ranks.

Fortunately, not only is traditional jujutsu still taught in Japan, but the headquarters of one such style was located only a fifteen-minute bike ride from our apartment. Thus my manner of entry into this particular system, the Hontai Yoshin Ryu, was so obviously fortuitous as to make me ponder such concepts as fate and karma.

The *honbu dojo,* or headquarters training hall, of Hontai Yoshin Ryu is located in a municipal building in Imazu, Nishinomiya. It utilizes this space with several other martial styles in an elaborate scheme of time-sharing. As it happened, the Japanese wife of an American who was an employee in the same firm as Surabela trained at the *dojo.* Shortly after our arrival in Japan, this family kindly invited us to their apartment, one similar to ours in a neighboring Sumitomo building. During a conversation over lunch there we discovered our shared interest in the martial arts, and I asked about jujutsu. The woman told us about Hontai Yoshin Ryu, and suggested I go see a practice session. She even offered to make the requisite introductions, highly significant in Japan. It seemed too good to be true. Barely containing my excitement, I thanked her for her offer, and made arrangements to go with her that very week to the *dojo.*

My first practice session in the Hontai Yoshin Ryu occurred less than two weeks after the date of our arrival in Japan. Hontai Yoshin Ryu is a *koryu,* or ancient traditional system, with both unarmed and weapons components. I began my actual training not in unarmed combat, but rather in the use of the six-foot staff *(chobo,* or *roku shaku bo),* since it was Tuesday night, when practice with that weapon was regularly scheduled. After the session, several of the group took me out for welcoming drinks and conversation. Although we had difficulty communicating (no one spoke much English, and my Japanese was still embryonic), we achieved and shared *kimochi,* the "good feeling" that is essential for group harmony in Japan. From such talks and shared training, strong interpersonal bonds were formed, and I was able to piece together some of the history and current state of affairs of my new style, a traditional school that has nevertheless changed to some extent with the times.

Although I did not know it at the time, the Hontai Yoshin Ryu, with some three and a half centuries of history, was actively engaged in exporting itself. It had already established several schools in Europe, and during my three year stay would establish others, including in Australia. No formal contacts had yet been made in the U.S., however. That several hundred students practice the style outside of Japan is ironic considering that a "crowded" night at the *honbu dojo* brings out perhaps a dozen participants, and most nights have fewer. In spite of the considerable foreign interest in the style, it remains relatively unknown among mainstream Japanese martial arts, and even more so in the U.S. Considering this, is it is again ironic, perhaps, that my three years of consecutive training at the *dojo* became the longest ever of any foreigner.

IN THE HONBU DOJO

The main training schedule of the Hontai Yoshin Ryu during my stay was on Tuesday, Wednesday, and Friday nights, from eight until ten. Tuesday was *bo* night, emphasizing the long (six-foot) and short (three-foot) staffs, while Wednesday and Friday emphasized primarily empty-handed jujutsu. The core of the jujutsu is encoded in sets of weaponless forms, or *kata,* including defenses against different types of attacks (for example, a wrist grab, lapel grab, punch to the face or body), and incorporates a variety of deflections, strikes, joint locks, and take-downs or throws. Additional jujutsu *kata* also include defenses against the *tanto* (knife) and *katana* (long sword), while other sets of *kata* involve the *wakizashi* (short sword), and the *hanbo* (three-foot stick), as well as the *chobo*.

Although I was generously offered the option of wearing my taekwondo black belt, I preferred to don (for the third time in my life) the beginner's white belt. The training suit worn in practice is a simple white *dogi,* with either a white or black belt tied around the waist. I found the pureness and simplicity of the unadorned uniforms and lack of colored belts to have a rather powerful and positive aesthetic effect. Occasionally in practice and always for demonstration purposes traditional black or dark blue *hakama,* skirt-like trousers, are also worn, which add considerable dignity to the outfit, but also require attention from their wearer when executing movements, particularly falls and rolls, since it is easy to get the feet entangled in the folds of material. Training is generally done barefoot, although for outdoor performances simple thonged *zori* (sandals) with or without *tabi* (split-toed socks) can be worn.

A practice session in Hontai Yoshin Ryu jujutsu is a curious blend of formal structure and informal relationships. Class is started and ended with students in a line, everyone seated in the *seiza* posture with feet tucked under (insteps on the floor and heels against the buttocks), facing the front of the *dojo* and the class leader. All bow to the front (where there is a Shinto shrine), and to the leader, who also bows; there may or may not be a period of meditative calm, *mokuso,* and some message or philosophical discourse by the leader. Inoue Tsuyoshi Munetoshi, the system's current and eighteenth Soke or Grandmaster, is particularly fond of sharing his philosophy. A lifelong practitioner of the martial arts and master of many styles (including jukendo, the fiercely competitive bayonet-derived style, in which he was two-time Japanese National Champion), Soke is an embodiment of the samurai ethos: disciplined, physically strong yet aesthetically sophisticated (a devoted practitioner of *shodo,* the way of calligraphy) and philosophical, successful in professional matters, and a socially prominent, leading citizen.

Whereas my first lesson in *bojutsu* emphasized basic striking movements with this weapon, my first jujutsu session began with *ukemi,* the all-essential break-falls that minimize risk of injury by helping absorb the shock of throws. We also worked some basic drills with partners that emphasized body mechanics, such as how a wrist can be extracted from a hand that has grasped it without applying aggressive force.

In general, warm-ups, following the bowing-in, are brief, usually only a series of front rolls back and forth across the *dojo,* sometimes followed by simple throwing drills. The greater part of a training session is spent practicing specific *kata* with a partner. The new student is introduced fairly quickly, it seemed to me, to the first and second *kata* in the first jujutsu series, called *gyaku no kata*. Unlike most karate *kata* or taekwondo *poomsae,* which are performed by individuals and can include twenty or more movements, jujutsu *kata* are practiced in pairs and may appear relatively simple: the attacker moves in (for example, grabs a wrist or lapel, or punches to the face or belly), and the defender responds with a designated technique. Correct technique and attitude, good timing, and proper body position and movement *(tai sabaki)* are of major importance. The defensive motion may be a locking or throwing maneuver with or without a strike, but is over in an instant, after which the two practitioners retreat from each other and take up a prepared stance in a state of heightened mind-body alertness called *zanshin*.

That all of this appears simple is what makes the actual performance of the *kata* so remarkably difficult. Jujutsu movements are replete with nuances and subtleties, and a type of body motion that must be cultivated over an extended period of time. Responses are typified by circularity and the use of the lever principle, and rely on a thorough knowledge of human anatomy for the application of accurate locks, throws, and even pressure point strikes *(atemi)*. Because true proficiency in this art requires not only refined physical technique, but a certain frame of mind, reflecting various qualities associated with the term *ju,* long and diligent training under expert instruction is required to attain it.

And so I began a new stage of my martial journey. In spite of my more than a decade of martial training, my initial progress felt agonizingly slow. Donning yet again the beginner's white belt in this different art really required me to "empty my cup" of prior conceptions, and to apply all of the glimmerings of awakening martial awareness in the study of this traditional Japanese system. All of my previously apprehended lessons of mastery were reiterated, and one utterly fundamental new one was added: the need for patience and the ability to flow.

Jujutsu is an excellent art through which to learn these lessons. Its subtle movements, timing, angles, and positions defy quick or easy acquisition, and its major philosophical tenet is *ju,* to flow, to develop and apply the qualities of flexibility and suppleness. Learning to flow with a partner, not to meet aggressive force directly with aggressive force but rather to use the attacker's own force, momentum, and position against him or her, has been an extremely important revelation. Ideally, once mastered, the skills of jujutsu allow one to neutralize an attack with minimal harm to oneself and with minimal expenditure of energy; they allow the smaller and weaker to overcome the larger and stronger; and they allow some degree of control over the damage inflicted on an attacker. Beyond this, the jujutsu adept can apply this concept of *ju* to interpersonal relationships of a non-physical nature, to reduce aggression and eliminate conflict. But of course all of this requires time, training, and patience.

PATIENCE AND FLOW

The Way to mastery is not a commodity that you can purchase at your local discount store, nor is it a refreshment or entertainment that gives immediate gratification. It is rather a series of challenges that comprise an endless process of being and becoming. Because this is so, and in spite of the many frustrations and setbacks you will inevitably experience along your Way, it is important that you acquire and practice patience. The development and application of patience is facilitated by an attitude of flowing with the Way. The more compulsively you struggle for achievement, the more you will become mired in frustration and defeat.

The self-discipline necessary to keep us on the track toward mastery despite setbacks, pitfalls, and endless frustrations can harden us to a point where we become physically, mentally, and emotionally stiff and rigid, as I discovered myself becoming in my earlier "crusty" phase. As one version of the *Tao Teh Ching (The Way of Life* in Witter Bynner's translation) puts it:

> Man, born tender and yielding,
> Stiffens and hardens in death.
> All living growth is pliant,
> Until death transfixes it.
> Thus men who have hardened are "kin of death"
> And men who stay gentle are "kin of life."

Over-rigidity is not only unattractive to others, but severely limits our development and abilities, and in a martial context can be deadly. In Eiji Yoshikawa's novel *Musashi,* our hero, the master swordsman, learns this lesson from Yoshino, a geisha he meets. Following a chance encounter, the highly cultivated Yoshino finds herself oddly attracted to this youthful and rather uncouth but impressive samurai. As they awkwardly interact, Yoshino reveals her sadness at Musashi's affected alertness and rigidity, which he defends by claiming to be in readiness to meet potential enemies. Yoshino counters by suggesting that while in such a state, if he were to be attacked in force, he would be killed immediately. The geisha illustrates her message poignantly, by cutting open the valuable stringed instrument upon which she plays so masterfully. She shows Musashi how the instrument's beautiful sound is created by combining its rigid wooden structure with flexible strings. Yoshino comments:

> . . . the tonal richness comes from there being a certain freedom of movement, a certain relaxation, at the ends of the core. It's the same with people. In life, we must have flexibility. Our spirits must be able to move freely. To be too stiff and rigid is to be brittle and lacking in responsiveness.

The geisha's message is that strength, hardness, and perseverance need tempering with gentleness, fluidity, and patience. This concept is actually incorporated in the name Hontai Yoshin Ryu, in which *yoshin* means the "willow heart-mind." In East Asian imagery, the willow's ability to bend in a strong wind is considered superior to the stiffness of the oak, which can be snapped off by the same gusts.

Musashi eventually became the embodiment of flexibility and flow, and shared this wisdom with his students and all of us in his creative works and writing. In the Water Scroll portion of his *Book of Five Rings,* for example, he condemns rigidity and praises flexibility: "I dislike rigidity. Rigidity means a dead hand and flexibility means a living hand . . . Always maintain a fluid and flexible, free and open mind."

By "letting it happen," as Master Hyong so frequently advised us, we are not so much in a rush to get to our objective that we make things harder for ourselves getting there. Habitually "letting it happen" will also facilitate the "letting go" necessary for ultimate mastery. Rushing headlong toward mastery will keep you far from it, like grasping for something in water, only to send it further away. Heedless haste distracts from the significance of the journey itself. Patience, the capacity of calm endurance, will help you measure your tread when you might otherwise recklessly dash forward, and can also help you tolerate the tribulations and challenges you will surely encounter on your Way.

EIGHT

PERSEVERE

Too early in the morning? Get up and train.
Cold and wet outside? Go train. Tired? Weary of the whole journey and longing just for a moment to stop and rest? Train. Continue on in the spirit of perseverance . . .

—Dave Lowry, *Sword and Brush*

I continued training in jujutsu and bojutsu at the Hontai Yoshin Ryu. Although at first unfamiliar and difficult, the smooth flow of jujutsu, as well as its inherent aesthetics, gradually became more natural to me. This process was greatly enhanced by training in a Japanese *dojo,* where there were many expert models to observe and mimic, and where my learning occurred in the rich texture of the total environment. Despite differences of individual expression, our sensei all moved with the same flowing mastery of the art, which does not overpower by brute strength, but rather uses momentum and minimal force expertly applied, delivered with great precision at the exact angle and point necessary to destabilize and ultimately immobilize an attacker. In bojutsu also there is a flow and smoothness, and although blocking techniques are not uncommon, evasion is a primary response to attack, with the staff, long or short, deftly penetrating an opponent's opening, or *suki.*

But as captivated as I was by this traditional system, and as patient and flowing as I was learning to be, I discovered that I needed more than patience to get me through day after day, week after week training in this challenging context. I needed a more dynamic quality that helped me get psyched for each day's training, and kept me enthused enough to go back the next time, despite frustration, confusion about technical points, and nagging injuries. My training required, in a word, perseverance.

Jujutsu training in Japan is serious, but at least the Hontai Yoshin Ryu is not run like a military drill camp. Nor is it particularly intended to condition the body for improved aerobic or anaerobic performance. It is primarily skill and spirit-heart training, and the master instructors who guided me did so expertly. Their method of training students is comparable to the steps used to forge a fine Japanese sword blade: repeated heating, folding, and pounding. I often felt that just as I was beginning to feel some sense of competence in a technique or set of *kata*, my sensei would identify a weakness and I would spend the rest of the training session, and often subsequent sessions, practicing the same form. Endless repetition and a concerted effort toward refinement yielded a sense of relative improvement; this was marked by the introduction of new forms to my repertoire and a growing confidence with the movements. But this relative improvement was punctuated by periods of confusion and even despair, when instructors forced me to reevaluate and significantly alter the performance of *kata* with which I thought I was already competent. This wave-like pattern of progress and apparent backsliding is utterly frustrating, but is tremendously effective in developing not only *waza,* technique, but such attributes of mastery as persistence, patience, and self-discipline, and nourishing the storehouse of these attributes, *kokoro,* the "mind" or "heart." Just as the repeated heating and pounding of the steel eventually produces the peerless *nihonto,* or Japanese sword, so through this process of struggle, confusion, and improvement can we forge stronger and more refined selves.

KORYU TRAINING

My concerns about being accepted as a foreigner in a traditional Japanese system *(koryu,* or *kobudo,* "classical martial style," as opposed to modern) turned out to be unfounded in the case of Hontai Yoshin Ryu. I was welcomed and trained like the other students, with whom I tried to blend in as much as possible. My training at the *honbu dojo* was guided primarily by Kanazawa Sensei and Yasumoto Sensei, both ranked at the *menkyo kaiden* level, or that of mastery in the art, and by Soke's son Kyoichi, and the other teachers, including Mitsuyasu, Sato (also *menkyo kaiden* at that time), and Soke himself. They would demonstrate a *kata* on me and on another student, correct my imitation of it, then gauge my progress in the form, providing me additional instruction when necessary and only introducing more *kata,* usually in pairs, when my competence seemed to warrant. I worked with a variety of *sempai,* or senior students, and over the course of my three years in the *dojo* became in turn *sempai* to my *kohai,* students entering the system and thus junior to me. Working with a variety of partners is important in jujutsu because each body is slightly different, and only through the repeated practice with an assortment of physical types can we master the instinctive, nuanced variation of technique suited to different physiques. And successful jujutsu depends on appropriately calibrated technique.

Training with the staff parallels this learning process. Training in the *roku shaku bo,* or six-foot staff, includes *kihon,* or basics, *bo awase,* or paired training between two *bo* wielders, and *bo kata,* which pit the staff against a sword. Here, skill is directly related to the amount of quality time a student puts into working with a staff, executing the basics, learning to flourish the weapon, and becoming familiar with its attributes for striking and defending at various distances and from different angles. To adequately feel the applicability of the forms, we would occasionally don protective equipment (essentially kendo armor, with additional shin pads) and spar with padded bamboo staves, or match staff against *shinai* (a kendo practice sword made of bamboo slats joined together). Again, the pattern of preliminary progress, setbacks, and eventual improvement was the norm, with Soke as often as not the principal instructor for staff training.

It was through this direct training under expert guidance in a traditional Japanese martial system that I began to understand more clearly the principles fundamental to cultivating mastery. In the constant training of basics, the focused effort and breath control, the disciplined yet flowing execution of increasingly aesthetic techniques achieved through the combination of steady patience and forceful perseverance, I could feel the true path of the warrior and the actualization of the principles of the Way to mastery of technique, form, and self. In their relentless quest for mastery, the *koryu,* or classical arts, proceed with the rigorous demands and effects of *seishin tanren,* or "spirit forging." And they tend to do so with minimal verbal instruction, preferring each student and traveler along the Way to realize the principles of the Way for himself or herself.

An important component of the traditional Japanese instructor-disciple relationship is *haragei,* or "belly talk," which stems from the belief that the *hara,* or abdomen, is the core of our being, through which we can intuit or otherwise come into direct communication with the thoughts or feelings of others. Much significant communication in Japan, at least traditionally, is perceived to take place via such non-verbal means, and such an empathetic bond is necessary for the successful direct transmission of knowledge that characterizes the classical arts systems, especially since much information is never verbalized or recorded. The degree of empathy developed in this intimate bond between teacher and disciple is even believed to be a revelation and a test of the depth of a student's commitment. This was something new for me, and it took me some time to understand that rather than having little or no philosophical emphasis, traditional Japanese arts and ways are in their very practice a living philosophy.

Also related to the seeming lack of overt attention given inner development in jujutsu is the classical nature of this art. In his seminal three-volume work on Japanese martial systems, *The Martial Arts and Ways of Japan,* the late Donn Draeger, who was actively teaching the Japanese some of their own martial systems at a time when most Westerners hardly knew such styles existed, devised a classification scheme that differentiates classical *jutsu* styles, which he translated explicitly as martial "arts," from *do* styles, or martial "ways." According to Draeger, the three primary considerations for what he identified as "classical bujutsu," or "martial arts," are in descending order of significance: combat, discipline, and morals; for "classical budo," or "martial ways," the three are morals, discipline, and aesthetic form. (I would suggest, although Draeger did not, that combat could be budo's fourth consideration, while aesthetic form might be the fourth for bujutsu.) Draeger further differentiates between these classical systems and what he identifies as "modern bujutsu and budo," these latter systems having as primary emphases (although not necessarily in this order): morals, discipline, self-defense, and health.

In other words, according to this classification, the aims of classical jujutsu were not concerned primarily with a philosophical dimension. However, to assume that the style therefore was designed purely for effective combat is to miss much of what is central to true Japanese jujutsu and other traditional arts. For combat effectiveness is believed enhanced by the cultivation of both *fudoshin,* the imperturbable mind, and *mushin no shin,* the mind of no-mind (concepts developed further in the next chapter), which are integral to mastery and go well beyond mere physical technique. Further, whenever dealing with things Japanese we need to be aware, as Draeger was, of differences between the overt and obvious, and those hidden or within, concepts expressed by such terms as *omote* or *tatemae* (the front, or face of things), and *ura* or *honne* (the back, or inner meaning). It is the inner component of classical arts that is their heart and mind (concepts that are regarded as interchangeable in this context), and it becomes the heart-mind of the ardent student who earnestly embraces and trains in such a Way. Depth of character and commitment as well as sensitivity are crucial to enabling the student to proceed from one level of perception and understanding to the next. Classical systems integrate mental and physical discipline with socially relevant concerns such as obligation, honor, and integrity. They were systems embedded in larger socio-cultural traditions which gave meaning to and reinforced the experiences of those who trained. Although classical systems are now taught in more modern contexts, there is yet much to be learned from them.

And yet, since jujutsu and bojutsu emphasize the cultivation of skill and spirit, I found my overall fitness and conditioning to be less than adequate. To improve this, I began to jog to and from the *dojo,* early enough to allow time to stretch before class actually began. Eventually I bought some dumbbells, and used these along with push-ups and other calisthenics for basic strength training. Although jujutsu does not rely on muscular force, or *chikara,* physical power is obviously an element in application. Excellence of technique sufficient to overcome brute force is emphasized, but where skill levels are equal, strength can often be the deciding factor. Strength is of various kinds, however, and jujutsu works to develop and focus the tensile strength of joints and connective tissue, as well as our inner strength or vital energy, *ki,* coordinating physical technique with energy through repetitive practice and breath control.

The rigorous practice of jujutsu results in strengthened joints and stronger muscle, although the hypertrophic bodybuilding physique is almost surely at a disadvantage in the performance of jujutsu. This is so because a reliance on muscular strength is counter to the very principles on which jujutsu techniques, tactics, and philosophies are founded, and also because large muscle mass can make the quick and subtle movements characteristic of jujutsu more difficult. It is not that a heavily muscled body cannot master jujutsu, but simply that it makes mastery more difficult. I found that the regular lifting of light weights combined with calisthenics and other strengthening exercises helped my jujutsu and bojutsu development, both by contributing to overall strength and fitness (which also generally helps mitigate the stresses of martial training), and specifically in reconditioning my wrist and elbow joints, which through the first eighteen months were almost chronically sore from training. Although I was not able to maintain my running schedule to and from practice, I did attempt to maintain aerobic conditioning by cross-training with occasional daytime jogging, solo taekwondo workouts, and aerobic calisthenics in my apartment, as well as by frequent bicycling and walking.

The combination in jujutsu of defensive joint locks and throwing techniques, combined with the traditional Japanese weaponry of *chobo* and *hanbo,* nicely amplified my previous taekwondo training in kicks and punches. But there was one more style that was necessary to round out my martial development, and that was training with the sword. Although we used wooden swords *(bokuto* or *bokken)* in paired forms with the *chobo* and *hanbo,* there was little in the way of formal sword instruction in Hontai Yoshin Ryu training during my three-year stay. Recognizing this, Inoue Soke strongly recommended that all students enroll in a class teaching a traditional sword style.

TOYAMA RYU IAIDO

Inoue Soke, eighteenth Grandmaster of the Hontai Yoshin Ryu, is also a senior instructor in Toyama Ryu Iaido, Yamaguchi-ha (the line of Toyama Ryu headed by Yamaguchi Yuuki, currently still training in his nineties). Iaido is not an easy term to translate precisely. All iaido styles derive from classical batto jutsu, where batto refers to simultaneously drawing and cutting or blocking with the sword. Although dictionaries commonly equate *iai* with *batto,* the two ideograms (for *i* and *ai)* that make up the former term literally mean "to exist," and "to join together, connect," respectively. Taken together, they can mean "happen to be present [at the same time or together]." In their book *Japanese Swordsmanship,* Gordon Warner and Donn Draeger take iai to mean that "the individual is possessed of sufficient inspiration, moral courage, and ethical timbre to unite himself with, and become one with, the cosmos." They go on:

> Iai-do is an art that enables the exponent to contrast the concept of "life" with a "life worth living." It is a system of character building . . . [and] its purpose, stated in the simplest possible terms, is to build a spiritually harmonious person possessed of high intellect, sensitivity, and resolute will.

Drawing and cutting with the sword is the overt, *omote* side of the art; uniting the self with the cosmos is its inner, *ura* dimension.

It seemed clear that to Soke both the technical training in
Toyama Ryu Iaido, and its underlying philosophy were important complements to what we were learning in the Hontai
Yoshin Ryu. (Since my stay in Japan, Soke has reinvigorated
the Hontai Yoshin Ryu by adding, or returning, complete sets
of individual and paired sword forms to the Hontai Yoshin curriculum itself.) And so he encouraged me to begin training seriously in Toyama Ryu, which I did in September, barely two
months after beginning in the Hontai Yoshin Ryu. My lessons
in Toyama Ryu began on Saturday mornings with personal
instruction from Soke himself in his own private *dojo,* located
above his family's living quarters and *sake* shop. This personal
invitation and instruction was extremely fortunate for me, and
was just one of the many kindnesses shown me and my family by Soke, his son Kyoichi, and other Hontai Yoshin Ryu
teachers and their families during our stay in Japan.

Toyama Ryu Iaido was developed around the turn of the
century and formed part of the training for Japan's military offi-
cers, ideally intending to combine both the Zen-derived philosophy of iaido with the battlefield competence of batto jutsu.
Reflecting this modern context, Toyama Ryu forms are performed standing, whereas older *iai* systems include or emphasize seated *kata.* The actual *batto,* or single-handed draw and
cut, is fast and explosive, while its full two-handed sword
strikes used to "finish" the imaginary opponent dynamically
incorporate arms, shoulders, torso, pelvis, and legs. Although
controlled, Toyama Ryu movements, when performed skillfully, are extremely powerful and awesome. The book *Naked
Blade,* by Toshishiro Obata, describes and illustrates Toyama
Ryu batto jutsu techniques that "are combat effective, yet dig-
nified, and ruthlessly efficient, yet graceful."

SPIRIT TRAINING

With the incorporation of Toyama Ryu Iaido into my martial
program, I could sense a maturing of my inner being, and the
deepening of my martial spirit. Since for the most part iaido
training is a quiet and calm endeavor, this may seem paradox-

ical. But these changes I felt within were due to the need to approach iaido training with whole-hearted sincerity and commitment: iaido movements must be clean, sure, and resolute. To achieve this, all principles of mastery must be cultivated and applied. Most critical is the repetition of relatively few and superficially simple basic techniques. Use of the *katana*, the Japanese sword, in Toyama Ryu is not fancy; parries, thrusts, and cuts are all fairly plain, overtly intended to efficiently and effectively dispense with the business of cutting down an opponent. But though superficially simple, the techniques yield new depth and nuance with each year of training.

The most difficult problem for me initially was the *noto*, returning the blade to the scabbard. Unless you have actually drawn and cut with a sword, you have probably never wondered about how it is to be sheathed again. The swordsmen seen in Western film, irrespective of style, generally look at their scabbard and sword as they bring the two together. But in combat, such an act could easily cost the swordsman his life; if one watches the sheathing motion, attention is diverted from other defensive activities. In Zen terms, the mind has been "fettered," or stopped at a specific place and time.

The Japanese swordsman overcomes this problem by maintaining an unfocused gaze forward, while executing the *noto* blindly. To do this, assuming one is right-handed, the left hand closes off the mouth of the scabbard in such a way that only the thinnest of openings separates the closed index finger and thumb. The dull back edge of the sword is then run over the meaty part of the hand between the base of the thumb and index finger until the very tip grazes over this part of the hand. At that instant the scabbard "captures" the tip of the sword, which is then slid with graceful control all the way in. Even though I trained initially with an *iaito*, or dull-edged (but sharp-pointed) practice blade, I found this apparently simple movement frustratingly difficult, and required repeated hands-on instruction from Soke. Training with a *nihonto* (a "Japanese sword," that is, one forged in the traditional manner) or *shinken* (a "live blade" with sharpened edge) is all the more challenging and rewarding. In fact it is said by purists that training with anything but a live blade is a caricature of true iaido, limiting personal development.

Most iaido forms include an initial one-handed draw and cut or block. (A thrust that may employ both hands is also possible.) This is generally followed with a two-handed cut, and always, before actually returning the blade to the scabbard, a focused flick *(chiburi)* that cleanses it of blood. These movement can be practiced separately—in Toyama Ryu, the major cutting motions are practiced in a sequence known as *iai kempo*—but all come together in the actual *kata.* Iai forms are short, but require tremendous self-control. Hasty movements, unbalanced form, and unsettled energy, negative qualities that would be deadly weaknesses in an actual battle, are starkly apparent in these short forms, and reveal the practitioner's level of development. Attention must be given to innumerable details, such as the proper sword grip, angle of the blade, angle of the cut, stance, breath control, and even direction of the gaze. Besides expert instruction, progress in this art requires countless repetitions of basic movements, and a capacity for sincere self-evaluation.

Kata is fundamental to Japanese swordsmanship. Everything of essence in iaido is *kata,* from the actual, formal movements, to the proper cleaning the sword after training, and even the folding of *hakama* and *dogi.* As I continued to train, I began to appreciate why form, and practicing forms, are so important. Form is critical because it patterns the mind and body to act most effectively, and does so along lines that are appreciated and thus desirable in Japanese culture. Besides effective technique, serious *kata* training helps develop self-control, attentiveness to detail, and a refined aesthetic sensibility. Commitment to form both in and away from the *dojo* contributes to the cultivation of personal dignity, and development of a nature that is respectful of and responsive to proper etiquette and social graces. When coupled with a persevering effort to go beyond our apprehensions about wielding competently a real sword, *kata* can also have a significant role in the cultivation of courage and the mind-set called *fudoshin,* the imperturbable, immovable mind. In short, in traditional Japanese martial and other artistic systems, *kata* is the foundation for total self-development and mastery.

Since *kata* is so fundamental in iaido, and since I had no previous formal iaido instruction, I needed more training than my weekly sessions with Soke. Unfortunately, the ceiling of our apartment was too low to allow for complete iaido practice, but I circumvented this to some degree by training in the *seiza* position. I also began attending the evening Toyama Ryu classes at the Imazu *dojo,* in addition to my Hontai Yoshin Ryu classes there. I practiced some of my forms, including the weapons forms (sword, and long and short staffs), in a neighborhood park, although I became increasingly uncomfortable with this activity since the sight of a *gaijin,* or non-Japanese, swinging around traditional Japanese weapons attracted too much attention.

While I admire expertly executed iaido of all styles, iaido cuts occasionally appear to lack actual cutting power. What Warner and Draeger say of modern iaido is essentially true: "Nor does any exponent of iai-do train himself to cut down any person or persons with his sword." What they mean is that in iaido the main target of the sword cut is our own baser self, and ultimately the whole ego, having as among its primary aims the cultivation of such Zen states of being as *fudoshin* (unmoving mind), *muga* (no-self), and *mushin* (no-mind). Nevertheless, an important way to develop the skill sufficient to cut down your own ego is by training to make actual effective cuts with the sword. Such skill requires considerable focus and technique, and it is precisely in the process, the Way, of mastering these that one ultimately "cuts down" the self.

For the most part, Toyama Ryu training is *iai kempo* and *kata,* but occasionally Soke would bring in green bamboo or rolled grass matting for *tameshigiri,* or "test cutting." It seems obvious that some physical contact with the sword blade should help improve technical competence, thereby positively contributing to those inner developments which are the focus of iaido training. Just like the taekwondo or karate stylist who tests himself or herself by breaking blocks or boards, test cutting is useful in iaido. Training kicks and punches in the air are important, but they must be enriched with the actual striking of more solid substance, to provide feedback on form and power, and to condition the various parts of the body to withstand the impact of actual contact. Ultimately, the focused breaking of boards and blocks, or the clean sword cut through some resisting material, provides vital information on our ability to coordinate the various components of successful technique.

As with breaking techniques in other styles, test cutting requires coordinated effort, including proper form, control of the breath, focus of technique and power, and the appropriate mental state. Proper technique requires not only that your movement describe the proper arc to and through the target, but also that the angle of the cutting edge to the target be correct. A good cut also requires execution with proper body angles and transmission of power to the blade on impact with a twisting or grasping of the hands, likened to wringing out a wet towel. It is important to achieve maximum power through correct form and speed, with focused tension or power applied only at the precise moment of impact. Not only will overly tensed muscles result in a slower cut (as kicks and punches are limited by tightened muscles), but will likely lead to improper cutting form or blade arc. Weakness in any of these areas can result in the blade failing to cut completely through the target; a poor cut, with ragged edges or a bad angle; or even a broken sword blade, an expensive and potentially dangerous problem.

For my first test cutting, I used an old *nihonto* that Soke kept as *dojo* property. My target was an upright length of green bamboo of about two inches in diameter that had one end impaled in a special stand. I was to use the classic *kesagiri,* a diagonal cut coming from overhead and proceeding at a downward angle from the swordsman's right to left. Ideally, only the forward part of the blade, known as the *monouchi* (roughly six inches back from the curve of the point) should actually make contact, and should cleave the bamboo at about a forty-five-degree angle. This was not only my first *tameshigiri,* but my first experience with a real, sharpened blade. As I drew it, I was immediately aware of its living edge. Not only was it heavier than my own alloy practice blade, but its wooden scabbard had been sliced over the years in many places through sloppy technique of beginners. Besides this, something in the glint of the steel, the line of its edge, and the sword's feel in my hand brought home the fact that I held an exquisite weapon of destruction.

Indeed, this idea of the life-taking sword *(satsujin no ken)* is what most people associate with this weapon and its use. But when guided properly, sword training also should inculcate a strong set of morals and personal discipline. These philosophical and even mystical associations with the refinement of self through sword training have given rise to the concept of a life-giving sword *(katsujin no ken).* Most associated with the school of Zen thought, this characteristic of the Japanese sword is beautifully described by the major Japanese spokesman of Zen to the West, D.T. Suzuki, in *Zen and Japanese Culture:*

> The sword has thus a double office to perform: to destroy anything that opposes the will of its owner and to sacrifice all the impulses that arise from the instinct of self-preservation . . . In the case of the former, very frequently the sword may mean destruction pure and simple . . . It must, therefore, be controlled and consecrated by the second function . . . The sword comes to be identified with the annihilation of things that lie in the way of peace, justice, progress, and humanity. It stands for all that is desirable for the spiritual welfare of the world at large. It is now the embodiment of life and not of death.

A blade with such power is not to be taken up lightly.

Of course, I did not stop to ponder all of this as I held the blade high and faced my target. In fact, I made an effort to suspend thoughts of any kind, drew in a breath, and stepped forward slicing out and downward while emitting a forceful *kiai.* I felt a palpable impact and heard a chopping sound, and the top third of the bamboo stalk fell to the floor. Good form had stabilized the force of the blow in my hips, preventing overcutting and falling off balance. And the cut was also fairly good, a little more acute than the ideal forty-five degrees, but straight, and with clean edges.

My feelings of confidence in the cut quickly faded as I faced the prospect of returning the razor-sharp blade to its scabbard without looking. As paradoxical as it sounds, keeping the opening between thumb and index finger small actually maximizes the probability of a safe *noto,* and although I performed it more gingerly than I was accustomed to doing with my *iaito,* it went smoothly. Soke next suggested I cut through once with the right-to-left *kesagiri,* then raise the sword and immediately cut through the remaining stem at the reverse angle. His quiet nod of approval after I was able to do so without mishap enhanced my sense of accomplishment. This brief but poignant experience demonstrated the significance of the live blade in the *seishin tanren,* or "spirit training," of iaido practitioners. Using such a lethal weapon in close proximity to your own body and those of others forces you to be focused and aware of every movement; ultimately, after persevering in your serious training, this focus and awareness should be a natural part of your actions, without the need for conscious direction. *Shinken training* dramatically enhances your potential for developing a resolute will and imperturbable mind.

Another notable element of spirit training in both Hontai Yoshin Ryu and Toyama Ryu was achieved via demonstrations. These were performed at various dates, times, and locations, the most important being on New Year's day at the Imazu Shinto shrine, when the various martial styles from the Imazu *dojo* celebrated a new year of life and healthful vigor by demonstrating their skills before the local deity and neighborhood. Performed in the wintry cold courtyard of the shrine, it was a wonderful celebration, helping to bring us closer to nature, to our community, and to the deeper significance within ourselves of our martial training. Other demonstrations were done as part of a larger program of either martial or other traditional Japanese arts, during intermission of martial competitions, or even as the special showcase event for some august gathering. With the eyes of spectators trained upon us, demonstrations were a fine opportunity to see how well we had learned our forms, and how far along we were in developing an ability to control or master ourselves, since a bad case of nerves would inevitably result in mistakes.

Since I was frequently the only non-Japanese participating in such events, I felt strong pressure to present the traditional arts I was learning as accurately and skillfully as possible. In one such demonstration, only several months after beginning my iaido training, I was a solo performer of several basic Toyama Ryu *kata* for a room full of local dignitaries. I felt it especially important in such a context for me to help achieve the primary objectives of these demonstrations, which besides being partially for entertainment, attempted also to educate the audience in their own martial tradition.

As an anthropologist I found this level of *participant*-observation, the hallmark of this discipline, to have gone beyond most textbook definitions. It also resulted in rewards far beyond the professional. Participating as a solo performer of a traditional Japanese art before a Japanese audience challenged and thrilled me. In our efforts to understand, interpret, and share knowledge about the diverse peoples and cultures around our world, anthropologists work hard to establish a rapport and a relationship of trust with those among whom we live and work. Through presenting to Japanese a demonstration of traditional Japanese arts, which are learned primarily through direct transmission from teacher to student, I was confirming my close relationship with the group, while their appreciation of my performance signaled their acceptance of me. I also felt that my performance of these arts was an affirmation of my appreciation of their beauty and power and, in some modest way, even a confirmation of their value to those who had created them.

JAPAN, A TOTAL LIFE EXPERIENCE

Although I consider my martial training in Japan to have been both intense and serious, it never exclusively dominated my life. Initially, family responsibilities, language and culture studies, and book writing required considerable time and energy outside of the *dojo*. And it was not long before even more responsibilities came my way.

In early March a blood test confirmed our suspicions that Surabela was expecting our second child. We were both euphoric and apprehensive. Since we were in Japan by the good graces of Surabela's employer, and since her pregnancy and the childbirth and subsequent child care would necessarily restrict her employment, we were concerned about our finances and the prospects of our remaining. We also had some concerns about having the baby in a foreign country, but these fears were allayed by research revealing that Japan is statistically one of the safest places on earth to give birth. Part of our dilemma was solved when Surabela's company agreed to keep her on part-time, at least to the end of her initial three-year contract, which also allowed us to stay in our apartment. And in relatively short time I was able to get a position as an assistant professor in the International Communications department of Otemae Joshi Daigaku (a private women's college). In addition to my Otemae duties, I offered a course on Japanese history to American college students attending the program that my wife had once attended at Konan University. My new positions brought additional income and significant new prestige, affording me relief from the quiet stigma I felt associated to my status as "Mr. Mom."

Our second daughter, Julia Paulina, was born with Japanese promptness on her due date in late October of the Year of the Dragon, in a Kobe hospital. We took her to our local Shinto shrine for the traditional infant blessing at one month after her birth. We were now four in our little apartment, but being a family, and having a baby in Japan, helped bring us closer to our Japanese neighbors and friends. When I started working, our older daughter Rebecca began attending a Japanese preschool (their only foreign student until her baby sister Julia joined her months later), and we became increasingly involved with activities there, as well as in neighborhood events, and programs at the *dojo.* My wife also began training at the *dojo* in Shindo Muso Ryu, which emphasizes use of the *jo,* a slender stick between four and five feet long. Although humble in appearance, this was the one weapon to either defeat or bring to a draw (the story differs depending on the teller) the great Musashi himself. Through involvement with these various groups we were able to observe and participate in a variety of *matsuri,* or festivals, and other Japanese traditional activities, such as pounding rice on New Year's day to make a thick, edible dough called *mochi;* pulling a *mikoshi,* a portable Shinto shrine; and training in *shodo,* calligraphy, the three-stringed shamisen, and the bamboo flute called *shakuhachi.* These experiences enriched us tremendously, and left us with a deep affection and regard for the many Ways of traditional Japanese culture, as well as the many Japanese we met through them. They also reiterated to me personally the need for balance in our personal development, and the common lessons learned by travelers on any Way of mastery.

PERSEVERANCE

If patience can be regarded as the passive quality of sustaining your commitment to your chosen path, then perseverance is the active quality of pushing forward. From an Eastern, Taoist-influenced perspective, calm, enduring patience, a passive element, is alone insufficient to the task. The soft and yielding yin must be balanced by a hard, forceful *yang.* Patience must be balanced by perseverance, the active principle of continually putting one foot before the other. Inevitably, you will stumble while on your Way. Frustrations will nag you, hurdles and plateaus will seem insurmountable, and your goals will seem chimerical, mockingly unattainable, distant and false. To some extent, patience can help you through such challenges, but only if appropriately supported with a will to actively forge forward.

In the Water Scroll of *Five Rings*, Musashi advises us: "You must walk down the path of a thousand miles step by step, keeping at heart the spirit which [you] gain from repeated practice." And in the opening quote to this chapter, Dave Lowry describes the attitude of *shugyo*, "austerity in training," linking it to the persevering spirit, a spirit that does not give up. To adopt this lesson for ourselves requires and develops in us true courage; it takes courage to continually face the challenge and rigor and pain of serious training, to frankly confront our deficiencies, to pick ourselves up after yet another fall, or to push forward after the umpteenth setback.

This is when calm and passive patience is simply not enough; it is when self-discipline and the fires of inner energies are needed to get us up and going further along the Way. In Japan, various forms of the verb *ganbaru* can be heard with great frequency. Although a dictionary may define it as "to stand firm," the forms of this verb are commonly used to exhort people to greater efforts, carrying such connotations as "Hang in there!" and "Be tough!," in a word, "Persevere!" It is inevitable that any Way to mastery will offer challenges that seem beyond our limitations. When facing these, there is one time-proven solution: train, persist, persevere.

NINE

CULTIVATE THE MIND OF NO-MIND

Whether your opponent is striking at you or you are in the attack, whether a person attacks directly or with a sword, whether during a pause or during the rhythm of fighting, if your mind stops even slightly . . . you will be killed by your opponent . . . The most important objective is not stopping your mind anywhere. If it is not put anywhere, it will be everywhere . . .

—Takuan Soho, in *Lives of Master Swordsmen*

The weeks and months passed rapidly, kaleidoscopic patterns of sights, sounds, smells, tastes, and textures, brought forth in bold relief one moment only to be scrambled and replaced by a new pattern in the next. There were my teaching and class preparations, writing and Japanese study, speeding to and from Osaka on crowded commuter trains, navigating through the maze of shops and streets of urban Japan, bike rides and park play, growing children to care for, worry over, and delight in, stolen moments with my wife, hot baths, tourist outings, television sumo and samurai, and training. On most nights I was either running, bicycling, or walking to and from the *dojo,* through the intensely humid heat of summer, and the dry cold of winter, throwing, being thrown, locking joints, dueling with staves, drawing , cutting and re-sheathing the sword, hammering out in the forge of the *dojo* a new and stronger spirit.

As I strove for mastery of technique, form, and self, I pondered why in Zen and Taoist sayings it is common to hear of the mind and skill of a master associated with that of the rank beginner, or even an infant. At first, given the long training required to develop mental and physical skills, these associations seem illogical. But if we approach the Way of self-mastery humbly and in earnest, the importance of the beginner's mind and the lack of contradiction concerning its similarity to the mind of the master become clearer.

Unecumbered with experience, lacking a developed ego, the infant's mind—the beginner's mind in the case of any totally new undertaking—is "empty," without knowledge and open to being filled with all possibilities. With its consciousness yet unripened and without the constraining know-it-all-ness of the "wannabe" expert, the infant/beginner's mind functions from intuition, instinct, and other capacities of the unconscious. It is precisely this unthinking mind that students of Zen and the martial arts seek, for such a mind not only leaves us less burdened with the desires and worries of the self, it also permits spontaneous response and action. With regard to technique, someone totally unskilled in defense faced with imminent harm may instinctively or intuitively apply a perfectly effective move to immobilize or escape from an attacker. This is possible because there is no confusion about what technique to use, or how and when and where to apply it.

As I was rediscovering in my jujutsu training, for the slightly experienced student of a martial art, all of this changes. From perhaps never having thought about what to do if an attacker grabbed here or punched there, the new student learns to position hands, feet, and body in specific ways in response to attacks, and to move and deliver techniques along certain lines, from specific stances, while maintaining attention to correct form and breath control. A student at this stage of development is in the worst possible plight, no longer able to respond from instinct, yet not skilled enough to put his or her new techniques into action automatically, without thinking. In such a state, one is all too aware of the conscious ego and its ideas, fears, and confusions. It takes years of sincere training to be able to develop the mind of the master, whether of martial arts or any other Way, which responds automatically and perfectly appropriately to any demand, whether willed from within or imposed from without.

Cultivating this imperturbable mind of no-mind and the clear mindedness that goes with it is what developing mastery is all about. It is the most challenging aspect, the most difficult to achieve and to apply consistently. As I gradually grew more comfortable with the empty-hand, staff, and sword forms of my training, I actively sought this mental state. But before I was really ready for it, the chance came to demonstrate my ability to control my mind and body.

THE FOURTH ALL-JAPAN CHAMPIONSHIPS IN TOYAMA RYU IAIDO

In the fall of 1989 it was announced that the Fourth All-Japan Championships in Toyama Ryu Iaido were to be held at the Hyogo Prefectural Athletic Hall, which was only about twenty minutes by bicycle from our apartment. Inoue Soke, one of the main organizers of the event, was enthusiastic, and busied himself with various details, including arrangements for some of his foreign students from Europe and Australia to attend. He made it known that every Toyama Ryu practitioner from the Imazu *dojo* was expected to participate.

I originally had no intention of participating; competitive athletics had long since lost all attractiveness to me. Even while competing in tackwondo under Master Ilyong's instruction, it was apparent to me that the ideal qualities of character cultivated in the training hall often seemed to fall by the wayside in the arena of combat, where the primary objective was to win, and not necessarily by displaying the highest level of skill. The atmosphere both in and out of the ring was often marred by egotistical pronouncements, self-aggrandizing actions, and inflammatory statements belittling opponents. It was incomprehensible to me that such discreditable deportment could be displayed by those who studied or taught martial arts, those who supposedly traveled the Way. How long before such competitors would use banned substances, if they were not already, to enhance their performances, or attempt to "take out" opponents by inflicting crippling injuries, all for the sake of winning awards?

Although I grant that not all competitors show such negative tendencies, I am not alone in these sentiments. Earlier in 1989 I had attended the First International Seminar of Budo Culture, hosted by Nippon Budokan (the governing body of all officially recognized Japanese martial arts) and the Kokusai Budo Daigaku (International Budo University). The main theme of this seminar of several days was to return the practice of martial arts and ways to a more traditional course of character building and moral development. Specifically mentioned in several papers presented by prominent Japanese scholars, the majority of them also long-time martial artists, was the lamentable development in character observable in many fiercely competitive practitioners of judo and kendo, which had developed in some quarters into martial sports, comparable to boxing, rather than true *do,* or Ways to self-mastery and spiritual enlightenment.

Once I began to absorb the physical techniques and philosophical tenets of iaido, I began to understand how my own ego, with its medley of bothersome thoughts, emotional instabilities, and sensual cravings, was the true target of my sword strokes and thrusts. Hence my surprise in hearing of competition in iaido, a style which ideally directs its practitioners toward egolessness. Proponents maintained that the competitive context was a challenge and opportunity for self evaluation, one through which personal growth could occur; competitors would train with greater focus than they might during the casual practice of every day, and would be able to benefit from the lessons learned about themselves in such a public and competitive forum. Implicit in this argument is the fact that swordsmanship was traditionally a means by which opponents settled claims and grievances through actual combat, and thus that training without some similar context of competition distances the style too dramatically from its heritage.

Perhaps these are sound arguments; they certainly support the view that the competitive arena has at least some place in the martial arts world. Some of these objectives however, could be realized through other means, such as intensive training sessions *(gasshuku)*, wherein a group of martial artists focus on body, mind, and spirit training in relative seclusion for a period of several days. Competition in practice can also provide such means, but need not require the singling out of winners and losers; in taekwondo sparring sessions, for example, students can pair up, spar for awhile, and then rotate or change partners without designating who has won or lost.

Regardless of my personal qualms, as a student of Inoue Soke in his Imazu *dojo,* I did not have the option of not attending and participating in the competition. In fact, Hontai Yoshin Ryu would be providing for part of the day's entertainment a bojutsu demonstration, in which I was also expected to participate. I resigned myself to the event, and although my training went on more or less as normal, there was some concentration under the tutelage of Soke's assistant Kurushima Sensei on the three specific *kata* that students of my rank, first-degree black belt at this time, would be expected to perform.

The competition took place on Sunday, and ran from nine in the morning until past five that afternoon. Hundreds of competitors from all parts of Japan, as well as a team from Taiwan, several Europeans, an Australian, and myself, all milled about the spacious gym until we were lined up for the opening ceremonies and things got under way. There were divisions by age, rank, and sex, and both individual and team competition, with various "matches" occurring throughout the gym. In each, three judges observed two competitors of equal rank, identified by strips of white or red cloth, perform simultaneously the prescribed *kata.* Red or white flags raised in the hands of the judges indicated winners, who advanced to the next round; losers were eliminated from the competition. My team of five of the Imazu students won our first round of competition but lost out in the second, and this was the only action I saw all morning, although around noon I participated in both an all-foreigner iaido demonstration, and a Hontai Yoshin Ryu bojutsu demonstration.

Competition in the largest category, that of adult male first- and second-degree black belts, began early in the afternoon.

Our group was so large that it was decided to divide it and run two simultaneous bouts before two sets of judges, with the victors of each of these two sections ultimately competing in a final run-off, judged by some combination of the two sets of judges.

Since even in competition iaido is performed at a relatively stately, controlled pace, including some abdominal breathing between *kata,* and since each competitor was performing three *kata,* this part of the competition lasted the better part of the afternoon. Two-by-two competitors stepped forward, bowed in, prepared themselves, and then executed their *kata,* bowing out after the victor was determined. I made an effort to enter fully into the spirit of things, managing through belly breathing and a conscious disciplining of will to maintain myself in as thought-less and ego-less a state as possible, with my movements as traditional and correct as my abilities allowed.

My first bout in the first round met with relative success; I won, two flags to one, but the center judge commented that my eyes were focused too narrowly and down. This needed correcting; raising of the field of vision to take in the total view both to the front and peripherally is considered the hallmark of optimal alertness for the swordsman. Obviously, he was also telling me, indirectly, that should this not be corrected in my next bout, it would be time for me to go home. This incident spelled out clearly to me how easy it would be to lose; a misdirected stroke, a wobble in the blade, even misplaced visual focus could terminate a competitor in this sudden death format. It helped steel me for more controlled effort.

Over the course of the afternoon, pairs of young and aspiring swordsmen continued to step forth and demonstrate their skill. I did not count the number of bouts, perhaps seven to ten, I actually competed in, for I was attempting to maintain a state of mind that was controlled and yet detached. About the time of the final bout in my section, the semi-final bout overall, Inoue Kyoichi suggested I try to relax, pointing out how I seemed too tense, too controlled. He joked about this later, mimicking my attempts to relax with shoulder shrugs and limbering up my face and limbs, holding this relaxed demeanor for a moment, then abruptly reverting to a kabuki-like caricature of my stern-faced and grimacing intensity of a moment before. Helped perhaps by this moment of levity, I was able to win this semi-final bout and proceed to the face-off between the victors of the two sections.

While appreciating my teacher's efforts, I was unwilling and unable to change my composure at that point. After all, I had made it to the final round of the competition, higher than any foreigner had previously achieved. And so, disciplined and intense, I stepped forward in the last bout, faced the judges, drew forth my sword, and with it my spirit, and cut through the essence of being. The judges observed in their inscrutable way, drew a breath, then snapped their little flags upward. I had won!

My *dojo* mates were quick to congratulate me, the only first place winner from our *dojo*. It was one of the most exhilarating and yet humbling experiences of my life. As far as I know, I am the first and only foreigner to ever win a category of this competition in Toyama Ryu Iaido, to be *yusho,* a champion. Certainly, my living in Japan and intensive training within the deep context of Japanese culture, as well as regular access to excellent instruction from expert teachers, gave me advantages over other foreign competitors. With this help I had fervently embraced my Way, taken responsibility for my actions, trained hard seeking aesthetic refinement, learned to control my breathing, and improved my focus and self-discipline, patience and perseverance. These actualized principles were leading toward mastery. Furthermore, one of the most important factors in my victory was my ability on that day to severely limit potentially distracting thoughts and emotions from disturbing me. That my mind was controlling my entire being became quite evident once I had actually accepted the fact of victory, and the end of the day's competition. Happening late in the afternoon, this realization came more than ten hours since my last meal, breakfast that morning. The moment I consciously relaxed this mental hold upon myself, my limbs began to tremble, I became flushed and broke out in a sudden sweat, and my stomach growled ravenously.

AFTERMATH OF VICTORY

Milling about after the award presentations, I passed by a group of Japanese who were discussing the day's competition. In passing, I noticed that the man speaking had been one of the judges for my section's bouts. Without intending to eavesdrop—he was speaking energetically, apparently unconcerned about who might overhear him, leastwise a *gaijin,* who are generally assumed to not understand Japanese—I soon perceived that he was speaking about the foreigner who had won the competition, me, and how that throughout the competition my eyes had been *kowai,* "frightening." He spoke of the powerful impression this had made on him. Although I took it as a compliment at the time, and although I acknowledge that the state of mind in which I competed was no small accomplishment, and certainly a crucial feature in my victory, I now know that it was not the ideal mind of Zen, not the imperturbable *mushin no shin,* "mind of no mind." I had a long way to go before attaining that level of mastery.

Musashi wrote the words about clarity of mind that introduce this book in the fifth and last section of his *Book of Five Rings.* This was his last literary work, written while he lived a veritable hermit's life in a cave shortly before his death at age sixty. The work was specifically intended to help his students learn more deeply the fundamentals of his Niten Ichi Ryu, but was also intended as a general guide for mastery of the self along the warrior's Way and what Musashi calls *heiho,* the Way of Strategy.

Musashi organized the *Book of Five Rings* into chapters, or "scrolls", based on the elements of the East Asian cosmos: earth water, fire, wind, and void. The "real emptiness" of which he speaks is the core of the short and final Void Scroll. This void, or emptiness, that Musashi associates with ultimate mental clarity and mastery is a concept derived from Indian Buddhism; it is a problematical one, and was as well for the early Chinese and later Japanese scholars who were confronted with it. D.T. Suzuki gives us some help in his insightful *Zen and Japanese Culture,* in which we find "emptiness" *(ku* in Japanese, derived from the Sanskrit *sunyata),* described as "the world of the Absolute," "formless," and "the fountainhead of all possibilities." The void, therefore, although without form itself, is the ultimate source of everything. Likewise, Musashi fittingly uses his chapter pertaining to void as the ultimate source of guidance to mastery of the Martial Way. The knowing of "real emptiness" that he describes is offered as the font of our own personal mastery, wherein our oneness with the void allows its limitless potential to be made manifest in our own being.

It is essential for anyone interested in the mastery of technique, form, or self to grasp—in fact to achieve, to be—the mind of no-mind, for the no-minded void is the ultimate source of creativity and right action. In this mind of no-mind there is freedom from conscious thought and from the desires of the self, states of mind which according to Buddhist tenets limit our development and lead ultimately to pain and misery. As Suzuki describes it, in the state of *mushin no shin,* "the body and mind are not separated . . . [and] move in perfect unison, with no interference from intellect or emotion." Intent becomes action, without any intervention from the consciousness of the thinker-doer.

The application of this state of mind to the martial arts is well explicated by the Zen priest Takuan Soho (1573–1645), a contemporary of Musashi, in his treatise *Fudochi Shinmyo Roku,* or "Record of Steadfast Wisdom and Divine Mystery." Takuan wrote this text as a letter to another great swordsman, Yagyu Munenori (1571–1646), who served as sword instructor and bodyguard to the third Tokugawa shogun. In Takuan's text, *fudochi* means "steadfast [unmoving] wisdom," and is related to the Japanese concept, *fudoshin.* This is a Japanese expression based on the Buddhist guardian figure Fudo Myo O, who is unflinching in his defense against wickedness. Figuratively translated, *fudoshin* means "unmoving heart-mind," and describes the imperturbability and courage of the truly mastered self. It is the heart-mind from which has been purged all impurities and weaknesses in the process of resolutely forging artistic and self mastery, resulting in an emotional and mental state unaffected by either external disturbances or inner desires. As Takuan explains, it is a mind that is "unfettered," one that is not caught up or distracted by phenomena.

To symbolize or illustrate this mind, Takuan presents the imagery of the Thousand-armed Kannon, Goddess of Mercy. If her mind were to stop to concentrate on the action of any one arm, the other nine-hundred ninety-nine would be useless; the image therefore represents the state of the unfettered mind, one able simultaneously and spontaneously to act in all and be in all one thousand arms. Such a mind is likened to the reaction of flint striking steel; an immediate spark is produced. Similarly, the mind that does not stop either in its own or an opponent's sword, or anywhere else, is able to respond with no time elapsed. With the conscious mind eliminated from the process, intention is action. This state of being is known as *muga,* "no self."

However, the mind that is tightly controlled to exclude stopping or concentrating on external distractions is not this mind of immovable, unflappable wisdom, even though it may superficially resemble it and may even enable a warrior to best an opponent. The clearest statement of this is made by the famous swordsman Yagyu Munenori, to whom Takuan addressed his *Fudochi Shinmyo Roku* text. In his Zen-inspired treatise on swordsmanship *Heiho Kaden Sho* ("Family-Transmitted Book on Swordsmanship," translated in Sato's *The Sword and the Mind),* written for students of the famed Yagyu Shinkage Ryu of swordsmanship, Munenori states: "No matter what you do, if you do it single-mindedly, trying to control your mind correctly and not allowing it to be distracted, you will end up becoming muddle-headed." The ideal mind, as described by this same master swordsman, who is said to have single-handedly cut down seven samurai who were attacking the shogun, is clearly described: "The mind of a man of the Way is like a mirror, because it has nothing and is clear, it is 'mindless,' and is lacking in nothing. That is the mind in a natural state. Someone who does everything with his mind in a natural state is called a master."

This then is the ultimate characteristic and criterion of high mastery, the imperturbable mind of no-mind, at one with and unfettered within a selfless self. While physical skill and mental concentration can lead you to victory, neither is the ultimate manifestation of personal development. Even Musashi, victor of sixty life-or-death duels before age twenty-nine, admitted that these victories were not accomplished with the proper mind or mastery of the Way, which he claims only to have achieved much later, at the age of fifty. If Musashi can admit to this, then how much more should we be wary of proclaiming our own "mastery"?

As far as the fierceness of my eyes is concerned, this also represents a stage or state of development that may be distant from the ideal. The most popular book accessible in English about *Musashi's* life, the epic novel Musashi by Eiji Yoshikawa, relates an early encounter in which the hero defeats one of the leading experts of the famed Hozoin spear style. As Yoshikawa tells the tale, it is the head priest of a neighboring temple, a Zen and martial master, who is able to truly perceive Musashi's abilities, and his weakness. Following the defeat of the spearman, this head priest summons Musashi and comments, "You seem to have the right attitude. But you're so strong! Much too strong! . . . Your strength is your problem. You must control it, become weaker." Reminiscent of Kyoichi Sensei's admonition to me to relax, this priest's comments indicate that even single-minded fierceness can be overdone. Although focus is fundamental to form and technique, intense, conscious concentration can be detrimental if maintained for too long a time. Besides requiring tremendous will, such heightened concentration also consumes a prodigious amount of energy, and leaves you less attuned to, and therefore more vulnerable to, other events going on around you.

Although fiercely applied mind-control helped me win a Japanese national championship in swordsmanship, it is not

the ultimate imperturbable and mindless mind of mastery. But
since that experience I have a stronger understanding of the
significance of mindlessness, and an internalized sense of the
mind that is unperturbed, unfettered, and unstopped by external phenomena and conditions. I am convinced that although
by no means easy, achieving such a mind does lie within our
grasp, by following the Way of centuries of masters before us
and earnestly and resolutely taking up the Way of mastery and
the nine lessons related here.

CULTIVATING THE IMPERTURBABLE MIND OF NO-MIND

The nine lessons offered are all fundamental to mastering technique, form, and self, but mastery is most elementally a state
of mind. It is the state of mind in which nothing separates you
from the direct experiencing of what you do, and from which
all clouds of confusion have been cleared away. But what really is this state of mind? Can you as the average person, without formally entering a Zen monastery or special training hall,
develop yourself productively and consistently towards mastery? How can we clear away the clouds that obscure from us
the essence of things, events, and even our selves? What can
help us to perform our tasks with grace and skill, and to act
with equanimity and integrity regardless of the circumstances?

Whether any of us will ever adequately or intellectually
comprehend what the state of mind of mastery is, the way to
it is neither secret nor distantly unattainable. Rather, it is a well-
defined path that has been followed effectively by others for
centuries, and lies open to us all. It is a path, revealed by the
nine lessons of Mastery, by which we forge courage, strength
of spirit, and a resolute will by repeatedly challenging ourselves to confront and go beyond obstacles that stand both
before and within us. And it is a path on which we learn by
repeated actions and training to loosen the grip with which our
consciousness holds us and all we do, replacing it with other
sensitive and perceptive dimensions of the mind.

When practiced regularly, repetitive training of technique
coupled with breath control will help us achieve the wakeful

state of mind in which conscious thought stops. This is the desired mind of *mushin no shin,* the mind cleared of all thought and the obscuring clouds of confusion. The more frequently we can achieve this mind, the less we will be fettered to distracting and confusing thoughts. Achieving no-mind in training and meditation will help us apply no-mind elsewhere, and can also help open intuition and other non-conscious sensitivities.

One advantage of achieving *mushin* is the ability to act with spontaneity and appropriateness. Coupled with *fudoshin,* by which we can act with courage on our convictions, this state of mind allows us to act and be in accord with our innermost selves. We are free to eat when hungry and sleep when tired; in other words, we are able to live an unfeigned and less complicated existence in accordance with the Way. And by clearing our perceptions and sensitivities of obscuring clouds, we gain a clarity of vision and understanding, of ourselves, of others, and of life, that is enriching and deeply sustaining.

The concept of *fudoshin,* an imperturbability of mind in a "mindless" state, is difficult for us to even imagine, let alone apply. But it is possible and accessible to us through training and attending to the nine lessons of Mastery. Recently, an international event of deadly consequence illustrated the applicability of *fudoshin* in the modern world.

On December 17, 1996, a gala gathering was celebrating the approaching holidays in Lima, Peru. Garbed in formal evening wear, the foreign ministers, diplomats, and other VIPs and their spouses basked in the warmth of fellowship and bounty. Sparkling crystal clinked in seasonal good cheer as the revelers toasted each other. Suddenly, an explosion shook the assemblage, bursting the dreamlike party image and replacing it with a nightmare, like the twisted plot of a cinematic thriller. Gunfire erupted stark and loud and was met by shouts and screams. The crowd of nearly four hundred people milled about confusedly. Doors burst open and shots cracked over their heads, sending the guests headlong to the floor. Armed and masked Tupac Amaru guerrillas swarmed through the luxurious residence.

"Everyone down," came a snarled command, "and don't raise your heads unless you wish them blown off!" Screams were nearing hysteria.

A guerrilla leader demanded silence, and the shots and shouts subsided, replaced by an electrified quiet punctuated with stifled sobs. Fatigue-clad men glared ominously over the inert horde, and then leveled their weapons at an unexpected sight: one VIP remained standing, visibly unshaken by the violent infiltration.

A rebel moved closer, shoving the smoking barrel of his gun towards the recalcitrant's face. "Who are you?"

The man faced both gun-barrel and glare without flinching. "I am Morihisa Aoki, ambassador of Japan." His voice was forceful and unwavering. "These are my guests, and they are unarmed. You will respect them and cause them no harm."

Awed, the guerrillas' eyes widened, and for a brief moment fingers tensed on triggers. But bold themselves, the guerrillas could admire grudgingly the courage of their captive. The rebel leader nodded. "All right. No one will be harmed." Guns were lowered, and an audible sigh spread among the hostages.

The scene I have just described is based on newspaper reports (particularly that of the Louisville, Kentucky *Courier-Journal* of Wednesday, January 1, 1997). Although I know nothing of the Japanese ambassador's past or training, it is clear that he is a man who has learned to govern his thoughts, words, feelings, and actions. He has learned self-mastery, and applied his *fudoshin* strategically and intelligently to help bring an explosive and potentially deadly situation under control.

Historical episodes that recount demonstrations of self-mastery and *fudoshin* in the face of impending death are especially numerous from Japan's feudal era (ca. 1185–1868), when the military class was politically dominant. One such tale concerns an encounter between two *daimyo* (generals and landowners), Takeda Shingen (1521–73) and Uesugi Kenshin (1530–78), famous for their fierce but chivalrous rivalry. Surprising his opponent during a battle, Kenshin drew his sword and prepared to cut down his disadvantaged foe, saying, "What would you say at this moment?" Shingen, facing imminent death with razor-sharp steel poised over his head, calmly answered, "A snowflake on the blazing stove," indicating the recognition of his own transient life. He then parried his adversary's sword cut with the iron battle fan in his hand, escaping what would have been certain death for anyone below his level of mastery. The source of this version of the tale, D.T. Suzuki's Zen and Japanese Culture, also tells the story of Zen abbot Kwaisen, who calmly lead his monks into a fiery death prepared for them by a powerful military leader. On the brink of the inferno Kwaisen declared:

> "For a peaceful meditation, we need not to go to the
> mountains and streams;
> When thoughts are quieted down, fire itself is cool and
> refreshing."

These models of calm leadership and courageous dignity are the direct application of *fudoshin*. The Japanese warriors and masters of old, in pursuing mastery of technique and form, recognized that such mastery was inextricably linked to mastery of the self. Not only is true mastery in the application of form and technique possible only with a deeper mastery of the self, but it is through the long and challenging process of mastering an artistic Way that the self can and must also be mastered. Resolve and courage result from frequent confrontations with and efforts to surpass our limitations and weaknesses. Long hours of focused practice with sword and staff, ink and brush, the implements of tea making, or even the delicate and varied stems of floral blooms, can all lead to the courageous resolve of *fudoshin*. By daring, time after time, to confront and exceed our deficiencies, debilities, and pain we forge a stronger, more resilient and less perturbable spirit. Traditional arts, learned in traditional ways—ways that emphasize long and rigorous training, the tempering of immediate wants and needs, and the internal fortitude to successfully meet and exceed these challenges day after day, year after year—are prescriptions for mastering technique, form, and self, and models for courageous living.

These are models we all need, and not only in times of crisis, but to bring dignity, rectitude, and honor to face the moral challenges, personal choices, and interpersonal relations and conflicts of our everyday lives. For most of us who are seriously training and traveling along our Way, such a state of imperturbable *mushin* is realized inconsistently, its coming and going a factor of our level of development. But our only option is to continue training, knowing that were we to actually achieve the every-minute mind of no-mind, we would *become* the thousand-armed Kannon . . .

When the mind is everywhere, it is also nowhere in particular; it has become one with the emptiness of the void to which Musashi refers in his *Book of Five Rings*. It is the unequaled state of mind and being with which to face either mortal combat or life in which misery and suffering otherwise abound. Those who achieve it are no longer controlled by a selfish ego, but are in harmony with themselves and the cosmos. They have achieved self-mastery, and are therefore beyond being mastered by others or by circumstances.

Concepts such as *mushin no shin* and void, and the paradox of a steadfast mind that is also unfettered and non-stopping, are not likely to be easily explained or grasped by our intellect. Fortunately, intellectual comprehension of these concepts is unnecessary for taking up a Way to personal development and mastery. A Way is a process, and what matters most is not the intellectual understanding of complex concepts, but the daily being and doing. If we proceed along our Way correctly and diligently, there *will* come mastery and perception without obscurity, the state of mind in which all clouds of confusion have cleared away.

FROM SELF MASTERY TO SOCIAL RESPONSIBILITY

Learning jujutsu is useful in defending yourself, your families and your country. It helps people keep peace. If your mind is following the right path of life, your martial art will be right. Respecting your ancestors, worshipping God and Buddha, having a thankful heart, living faithfully and working honestly for others are essentials of your life and Hontai Yoshin Ryu.

—Inoue Tsuyoshi Munetoshi, *Eighteenth Soke, Hontai Yoshin Ryu*

A number of years have come and gone since our return to the U.S. from Japan. While I teach anthropology at a small college and share what I can of my time with my family, my quest for mastery, of technique, of form, and of self, continues with its challenges, frustrations, and occasional glimpses of clarity. Teaching and researching in anthropology remain my formal profession, now inextricably intertwined with my martial avocation. Martial training continues to be my chosen Way, and as I journey along it, I strive to offer what I think I know and have learned with others I meet.

My daily life both applies and challenges the personal growth and wisdom, self-control and sought-after mastery of my martial training. As a professor, my workday extends into evening and weekends with course preparation, reading, grading, research, writing and a host of administrative tasks. Also, our family has grown—Alexander Carvalho joined us in 1994— and makes its own demands on my time, energy, and affection. As my wife also pursues a professional career and her own personal development, so we endeavor everyday to coordinate schedules, share time, and retain our sanity.

In the maelstrom of activity we call modern living, with our multiple roles and their concomitant responsibilities, the regularity and personal forging of a chosen Way can be a stabilizing and empowering force in our lives. It can help us, if imperfectly, to clear away and see through some of the clouds that confuse and confound us. And it can help us achieve and actualize potential that is not only beneficial and applicable in our own lives, but which we can then put to use on behalf of others.

MASTERY AND SOCIAL OBLIGATION

Speaking as I have been in previous chapters of a state of being that is likened to "emptiness," a heart-mind that is "unmoving" or "unfettered" can be perplexing, and can seem to describe an amoral or asocial personality. But such is not the ideal individual sought by East Asian systems of mastery. Buddhism, the philosophical tenets of which influence so many formal Asian Ways of mastery, is a profoundly moral way. In addition, Chinese Ch'an and Japanese Zen Buddhism were cultivated and grew in societies where the social fabric was woven on the loom of Confucian ethics, which emphasize social etiquette, obligation to others, and a submersion of self interest in favor of the group. Whether we are living in a medieval or feudal society, or in the contemporary era of "postmodern" liberal democracy, mastery is desirable precisely because we are social beings living in an interactive and social universe.

Many arts of East Asian origin have integrated within them a concern for balanced physical, mental, and socially-relevant moral development. For example, in China, the hearth for much of East Asia's martial development, fighting systems known collectively today as *kung fu* were generally associated with moral precepts and the inner being. In their book *Kung Fu,* David Chow and Richard Spangler summarize the philosophical essence of *kung fu:* "Learn the ways to preserve rather than destroy. Avoid rather than check; check rather than hurt;

hurt rather than maim; maim rather than kill; for all life is precious, nor can any be replaced."

Chinese styles are typically imbued with holistic philosophies. They combine physical training with *ki* development and breath control, and healing knowledge and practices, and generally strive for an overall balance between personal development and social responsibility. These qualities of character can even be found in great military leaders. In the *Arts of War,* the 2500-year old masterwork of military strategy ascribed to Sun Tzu, the successful general is defined as one possessing such socially relevant qualities as sincerity, humanity, and wisdom, in addition to the more militarily useful traits of courage and discipline. In fact, all of these traits would enhance everyday life in any society.

As discussed in chapter 2, Korean styles trace their inspiration to the institution of the *hwarang,* youths of the nobility who were trained in both martial and cultural arts, with an emphasis on the moral principles of loyalty, filial piety, trustworthiness, courage, and justice. *Hwarang*-inspired styles emphasize a rounded development, striving for personal and leadership skills that will promote an enlightened and harmonious society.

Among the Japanese, the *bushi,* or warrior class set much of the tone for social development and standards during the nation's long feudal period (from ca. AD 1200 to the mid-nineteenth century). While there were differences over time and among various feudal fiefdoms as well as gross deviations from the ideals of Japanese-defined chivalry, in general the code of honor and behavior of the samurai was one of high moral principle. In his work *Bushido,* Nitobe describes the ideal code as characterized by the following "pervading characteristics": rectitude or justice (including the concept of *giri,* which came to be understood as duty or obligation "to parents, to superiors, to inferiors, to society at large"), courage, benevolence, politeness, sincerity, honor, loyalty, and self-control. He goes on to say:

> A samurai was essentially a man of action . . . *Bu-shi-do* means literally Military Knight Ways—the ways which [samurai] should observe in their daily life as well as in

their vocation . . . The tripod which supported the framework of Bushido was said to be *Chi, Jin, Yu,* respectively, Wisdom, Benevolence, and Courage.

The application of these characteristics was furthermore based on interpretations of important classical Chinese writings, including those of Confucius, Mencius, and others. The result of this code was a highly structured society based on patterned form, *kata* or *shikata,* with behavior and motivations resting on strong ethical underpinnings.

And in Okinawa, as described by Funakoshi Gichin, who introduced the world-renowned art of karate from that island to the main island of Japan, there was traditionally an ideal emphasis on humility and just action. As Funakoshi explains in his inspirational autobiography *Karate-Do: My Way Of Life*:

> There is a Buddhist saying that "anyplace can be a *dojo,*" and that is a saying that anyone who wants to follow the way of karate must never forget. Karate-do is not only the acquisition of certain defensive skills but also mastering the art of being a good and honest member of society.

Throughout pre-modern East Asia, therefore, we see that social life was ideally highly ethical, if also highly structured, and that traditional martial systems helped promote and reinforce prevailing social standards in the training of their adherents. While contrary examples abound, there was in traditional East Asia a strong core of exemplary ethical behavior, with stunning examples of personal and artistic mastery. Countless lines of inspired poetry; innumerable masterpieces in brush, ceramics and sculpture; breathtaking theatrical performances; and the very lives and teachings of historical figures such as Musashi, Takuan, Yagyu Munenori, and others all testify to the viability and success of carefully cultivated Ways to mastery.

MASTERY AND MODERN TIMES

While the West certainly also has its ideal moral and ethical way and its masters and masterpieces, contemporary socio-cultural developments nevertheless have resulted in confused and confusing values, as well as high levels of stress, crime, and violence. In some parts of the United States and elsewhere in the industrial and urbanized world, drug use and abuse is out of control, sexually transmitted diseases are epidemic, and crime, especially of a violent nature, is rampant. Young people are forced by relentless peer pressure to conform to values that are blatantly and harmfully deviant by traditional standards, resulting in record cases among the young of substance abuse, violence, and delinquency, as well as psychologically related illnesses such as bulimia, anorexia, and depression, often leading to suicide.

We live in a highly technological society, where instant gratification and quick and tangible rewards are expected; where there is an ever-increasing emphasis on materialism, consumerism, and the narcissistic individual; where individual rights are touted, but personal responsibilities are all but forgotten. Self-indulgence, self-enrichment, and self-satisfaction are flaunted as acceptable goals, with the exploitation of others the inevitable result. Even the natural environment is ravaged, polluted, and made a commodity. It is an era in which the pace of change has outstripped that of any prior period, and when in fact change, implemented by robust departments of research and development, has become a way of life contributing greatly to social anomie and the loss of self. What contemporary Western society needs is help in developing strength and depth of character, self-control, and personal discipline.

Rather than wait, hoping for someone else or government-driven social reforms to alleviate contemporary social woes, each individual could help effect dramatic improvements in modern living by striving to attain the clarity and imperturbability of mind and mastery of technique, form, and self that come through the pursuit of an earnestly embraced Way. Even without total mastery, the serious effort, especially in systems of East Asian origin or inspired by them, could make positive social contributions. How? Overtly, such efforts require us to apply our time and energy in constructive and positive ways, therefore logically reducing the potential for more destructive pastimes. Perhaps less obvious but no less relevant, the moral and philosophical tenets which underlie East Asian systems of personal development emphasize the fundamental norms and mores upon which the broader society in which these systems exist is founded. Traditionally, these norms and mores de-emphasize the individual, and stress the obligations and responsibilities of persons as participating members of larger social groups. Self-development is sought in order to maximize our personal potential, not for our own personal gain or self-aggrandizement, but rather to provide us with more to offer the larger community.

Traditional instruction in all Ways, martial and otherwise, centers upon countless repetitions of basic movements. Motions are generally patterned into forms, which are prac-ticed individually or as a group, with or without partners. Aesthetic mastery of technique is fundamental to these sys-tems. The emphasis on form and repetition ideally builds the student's patience and endurance, enhances loyalty and respect, deepens humility and self-knowledge, and when per-formed in a group, develops important social skills and aware-ness of social responsibilities. The long, tedious process of training can naturally cultivate a patient and persevering spirit, and can therefore help counter a need for instant gratification and immediate, tangible rewards. Learning directly from those more skilled than us helps instill humility and respect, and training a group, which often comes to be considered as a "family," emphasizes loyalty, proper etiquette, and appropri-ately moral conduct (especially since consequences for the immoral conduct of one member of a group would reflect neg-atively upon the entire group). Furthermore, the simple basics of many traditional systems often require little space or special equipment, which can offset contemporary materialistic and consumer dependencies. Moreover, the continuous rigor of training, of facing our fears, weaknesses, pains and incompe-tence and working to overcome them, helps to instill courage,

courage with which we can stand up to peer pressure and destructive influences and dare to try making a positive contribution to our world.

Problems with anomie and alienation so common in our fast-changing world can be reduced through a training process that contributes to our knowledge of self and our relationship to others, and by repeated basics that are carried along and built upon over the years, providing a base from which to develop and to which we can regularly return. This results in an overall continuity of self, even amidst other changes in our lives. Although knowledge of the self is enhanced in traditional, artistic systems, there is no room for shallow ego-centrism. Rather, especially through working with others, knowledge of and sensitivity toward our fellow human beings is enhanced, along with self-control, coordination, and a sense of cooperation. The self and individuality can and should be cultivated, trained, and mastered, not for self-glorification, but so as to be able to do and give more, and more ably, to others.

All of us can strive to better ourselves and our world. These are not new goals, and many methods have been devised to achieve them. Wholeheartedly embracing an artistic Way and working toward its mastery is particularly noteworthy in this regard. To truly master such a Way, we must also ultimately master ourselves. And for those who have ever lost emotional control and regretted it, or have been unable to respond mentally or physically as they wished, or have had decisions controlled by self doubts, fears, and anxieties, then the appeal of self-mastery should be obvious.

Paradoxically, attempts at self-mastery and mastery of an artistic Way actually requires a diminishing of ego. As we strive to develop our self, we in fact must diminish self-importance. How can we do this? Since mastery is achieved partially through a reduction of conscious thought, and since our ego is maintained primarily through our conscious intellection and the construction of self that accompanies this process, the diminishing of self-importance will occur naturally while treading the Way of mastery.

An important component of mastery and diminishing of the self is our start at humble beginnings. When beginning to learn any new skill, our ignorance and incompetence are often glaring, especially when compared with the abilities of our teachers. Humility and appreciation for the talents of others becomes the basis for respect; humility and respect together help lower our evaluation of our own importance, and can help develop our ability to empathize with those around us. Empathy enhances our ability to harmonize with our surroundings and the task at hand. With empathy the artist becomes the bamboo so masterfully painted in black washes on white, the florist becomes the arrangement of flowers, the master dancer is the dance. And as we proceed along our chosen Ways, we need to remind ourselves to try to keep the freshness of the beginner's mind and its associated benefits.

By reducing the significance of our conscious self, of ego, we can be the thousand-armed Kannon, with each arm fully capable of independent action because our mind, stripped of the shackles of conscious identity, is able to be nowhere and everywhere at once. With no-ego *(muga),* as with no-mind *(mushin),* intent becomes action, art is artless and flows from a selfless self, and the sword used to take life becomes one that gives life. This is the heart of the Way, the essence of mastery.

CLEARING AWAY CONFUSION

There are many visions and definitions of what constitutes a meaningful life, of the path personal development should take. But as aikido founder Ueshiba Morihei put it in *Budo: Teachings of the Founder of Aikido:* "The Path is exceedingly vast. From ancient times to the present, even the greatest sages were unable to perceive and comprehend the entire truth . . . It is not possible for anyone to speak of such things in their entirety." Each of us can and should strive for our own personal knowing of the Way.

From one perspective, mastery of a skill is simply a tool or mechanism useful for mastering the self. Mastery of the self is perhaps in its turn but a tool or mechanism for arriving at some other level of development. For example, Musashi himself spoke of the possible attainment of "supernatural powers" through daily and deeply committed striving along the Way. Whatever your target or ultimate goal, it is clear that self-mastery and optimal personal growth go hand-in-hand, with clearing away the clouds of confusion a natural process of any fully embraced and sincere path of personal development.

The clouds that obscure our vision and confuse our thoughts and actions come from our own cognitive processes, conditioned to respond to external and internal stimuli. Every waking minute of everyday stimuli bombard our senses and cognition, with prescribed or desired patterns of perception and response developed by personal preferences and the various forces of enculturation and socialization. Under such a blitz of information and stimulation and influential external control we generally shuffle and stumble our way through a maze of demands, expectations, and desires. Consternated and befuddled, we become lost.

In such a milieu, true personal development—the forging of our spirits, the cultivation, strengthening, and growth of our total being—will be sporadic if it occurs at all. We need a way out of the maze. But rather than seeking such an escape among the confusing morass of external goings on, we should realize that the way out actually lies within.

We can clear away these confusing clouds by stripping away the artifice of who we are made to think we are, and by cultivating a spirit detached from transient and trivial concerns. A serious effort at self-cultivation by learning and applying the nine lessons of mastery as presented here can help us achieve clarity of mind and purpose. This is our key to resolving the human dilemma.

Each of us is a unique human being, the product of innate biological programming and spiritual essence nurtured by our social and natural environment. And we are each best positioned to know who we are, as we are the closest to ourselves. Self-knowledge is integrally associated with self-mastery, and setting these as goals is the only effective way out of the maze.

By embracing an artistic Way and applying ourselves to the principles of mastery in its undertaking, we will learn not only new technique and form, but also about ourselves and others. We are necessarily helped along this Way by many teachers, guides who in one way or another hold out their hands, catch us as we stumble, help disperse our clouds of confusion, and direct us to new phases of growth. In turn, we must also be ready to share of ourselves with others, through our improved clarity of vision and understanding judiciously helping, guiding, supporting, and letting go, so that others can achieve more of their potential mastery of technique, form and self. And so the cycle continues . . .

In the introductory quote to this book, Miyamoto Musashi observes that through training "one should know real emptiness as the state where there is no obscurity and the clouds of confusion have cleared away." "Real emptiness" is achieving the imperturbable mind of no-mind, *mushin no shin.* It is truth, an ego-less state of primal essence, and it is in this state where self-knowledge and self-mastery fuse with pure being and we achieve oneness with self and the Tao, the immutable Way of life itself. In this state "there is no obscurity" for "the clouds of confusion have cleared away." Echoing Musashi's words centuries later, the great twentieth-century martial artist Ueshiba admonishes us to "Always keep the mind as bright and clear as the vast sky."

Perhaps achieving this bright clarity of non-thinking essence and maintaining it perpetually as our normal state is not possible for all; perhaps such every-minute "emptiness" does not even sound particularly desirable. Be that as it may, we all can benefit from less confusion in our lives, and the most effective way to achieve this is to take up a Way, any Way, as our serious undertaking, applying the lessons for mastery offered here. As a process, actively seeking mastery goes on, a lifelong quest. And in the striving toward mastery, we achieve a depth, a richness, a quality of life not commonly experienced, and so enhance the quality of life of all around us. Once you experience this, you will begin to know more of yourself and of others. You will begin to see more clearly: the clouds of confusion will clear away!

[Train] intently with your entire mind and body, temper yourself ceaselessly, and advance on and on; weld yourself to heaven and earth and unify practice and enlightenment. Realize that your mind and body must be permeated with the soul of a warrior, enlightened wisdom, and deep calm.

—Ueshiba Morihei,
Budo: Teachings of the Founder of Aikido

BIBLIOGRAPHY

The following list includes many of the resources I have read over the years that have been helpful in my personal and martial development. It is certainly not exhaustive of the relevant material in print, but I hope that it can prove interesting to at least some readers. In addition to books, the journals *Furyu* and the *Journal of Asian Martial Arts* are reliable sources of information and inspiration.

Braverman, Arthur, ed. *Warrior of Zen.* New York: Kodansha International, 1994.

Cho, Hee Il. *Man of Contrasts.* Cho's Taekwon-Do Center, 1977.

Chow, David and Richard Spangler. *Kung Fu: History, Philosophy and Technique.* Burbank: Unique Publications, 1982.

Chun, Richard. Tae Kwon Do: *The Korean Martial Art.* New York: Harper and Row, 1976.

Confucius. *The Analects.* D.C. Lau, trans. New York: Viking Penguin, 1979.

Daidoji, Yuzan. *Budoshoshinshu.* 1. William Scott Wilson, trans., as *Budoshoshinshu: The Warrior's Primer.* Burbank: Ohara Publications, Inc., 1984. 2. A.C. Sadler, trans., as *The Code of the Samurai.* Tokyo: Charles E. Tuttle, 1941.

Deshimaru, Taisen. *The Zen Way to the Martial Arts.* New York: E.P. Dutton, 1982.

Donohue, John J. *The Forge of the Spirit.* New York: Garland Publishing, Inc., 1991.

Draeger, Donn F. "The Martial Arts and Ways of Japan," Volume 1: *Classical Bujutsu* (1973); Volume 2: *Classical Budo* (1973); and

Volume 3: *Modern Bujutsu and Budo* (1974). New York: Weatherhill.

Draeger, Donn F. and Robert W. Smith. *Comprehensive Asian Fighting Arts*. New York: Kodansha International, 1980 (1969).

Draeger, Donn F. and Gordon Warner. *Japanese Swordsmanship*. New York: Weatherhill, 1982.

Funakoshi, Gichin. *Karate-Do: My Way of Life*. New York: Kodansha International, 1975.

Furuya, Kensho. *Kodo: Ancient Ways*. Burbank: Ohara Publications, Inc., 1996.

Gluck, Jay. *Zen Combat*. Ashiya, Japan: Personally Oriented Books, 1996.

Heckler, Richard Strozzi. *In Search of the Warrior Spirit*. Berkeley: North Atlantic Books, 1990.

Herrigel, Eugen. *Zen in the Art of Archery*. Translated by R.F.C. Hull. New York: Random House, Vintage Books, 1953.

Hyams, Joe. *Zen in the Martial Arts*. New York: Bantam Books, 1979.

Institute for Zen Studies. *How to Practice Zazen*. Kyoto, n.d.

Lao Tzu. *The Way of Life (Tao Te Ching)*. Witter Bynner, trans. New York: Perigee Books, 1972 (1944). Also in Chinese Mystics, Raymoond Van Over, ed. New York: Harper and Row, 1973.

Lee, Bruce. *Tao of Jeet Kune Do*. Burbank: Ohara Publications, Inc., 1975.

Lee, Joo Bang. *The Ancient Martial Art of Hwarang Do*. Burbank: Ohara Publications, Inc., 1978.

Lowry, Dave. *Autumn Lightning:* The Education of an American Samurai. Boston: Shambhala, 1985.

_____. *Sword and Brush: The Spirit of the Martial Arts.* Boston: Shambhala, 1995.

Miyamoto, Musashi. *Go Rin no Sho [A Book of Five Rings].* 1. Victor Harris, trans. Woodstock, NY: Overlook Press, 1974. 2. Nihon Services Corporation, trans. New York: Bantam Books, 1982. 3. Thomas Cleary, trans. Boston: Shambhala, 1993.

Morgan, Forrest E. *Living the Martial Way.* Fort Lee, NJ: Barricade Books, 1992.

Morris, Vince. Zanshin: *Meditation and the Mind in Modern Martial Arts.* London: Samuel Weiser, Inc., 1992.

Nicol, C.W. *Moving Zen: Karate as a Way to Gentleness.* New York: Quill, 1982.

Nitobe, Inazo. *Bushido: The Soul of Japan.* Tokyo: Charles E. Tuttle, 1969 (1905).

Norris, Chuck. *The Secret Power Within: Zen Solutions to Real Problems.* Boston: Little, Brown and Co., 1996.

Ochiai, Hidy. *Hidy Ochiai's Living Karate.* Chicago: Contemporary Books, 1986.

Obata, Toshishiro. *Naked Blade: A Manual of Samurai Swordsmanship.* Tiptree, Essex, UK: Dragon Books, 1985.

Quinn, Cameron. *The Budo Karate of Mas Oyama.* Brisbane, Australia: Coconut Productions, 1987.

Ratti, Oscar and Adele Westbrook. *Secrets of the Samurai.* Tokyo: Charles E. Tuttle, 1973.

Sato, Hiroaki. *The Sword and the Mind.* Woodstock, NY: Overlook Press: 1985.

Sekida, Katsuki. *Zen Training: Methods and Philosophy.* New York, Weatherhill: 1975.

Shim, Sang Kyu. *Promise and Fulfillment in the Art of Tae Kwon Do.* Detroi, 1974.

————— . *The Making of a Martial Artist.* Detroit, 1980.

Skoss, Diane, ed. Koryu Bujutsu: *Classical Warrior Traditions of Japan.* Berkeley Heights, NJ: Koryu Books, 1997.

Soho, Takuan. *The Unfettered Mind.* William Scott Wilson, trans. New York: Kodansha International, 1986.

————— . "Fudochi Shinmyo Roku." 1. Sato Hiroaki, trans., in *The Sword and the Mind.* 2. William Scott Wilson, trans., in *The Unfettered Mind.* 3. Sugawara Makoto, trans., in *Lives of Master Swordsmen.* 4. D.T. Suzuki, trans., in *Zen and Japanese Culture.*

Stevens, John. *The Sword of No-Sword: The Life of the Master Warrior Tesshu.* Boston: Shambhala, 1994.

Sugawara, Makoto. *Lives of Master Swordsmen.* Tokyo: The East Publications, 1985.

Suino, Nicklaus. *Arts of Strength, Arts of Serenity.* New York: Weatherhill, 1996.

Sun Tzu. *The Art of War.* 1. Samuel B. Griffith, trans. Oxford: Oxford University Press, 1963. 2. Thomas Cleary, trans. Boston: Shambhala, 1988.

Suzuki, D.T. *Zen Buddhism: Selected Writings.* William Barrett, ed. Garden City, NY: Doubleday Anchor Books, 1956.

_____. *Zen and Japanese Culture.* Princeton: Princeton University Press and the Bollingen Foundation, NY, 1959.

Tohei, Koichi. *Book of Ki.* Tokyo: Japan Publications, Inc. 1976.

Ueshiba, Kisshomaru. *The Spirit of Aikido.* Translated by Taitetsu Unno. New York: Kodansha International, 1984.

Ueshiba, Morihei. Budo: *Teachings of the Founder of Aikido.* John Stevens, trans. New York: Kodansha International, 1991.

Westbrook, Adele and Oscar Ratti. *Aikido and the Dynamic Sphere.* Tokyo: Charles E. Tuttle, 1970.

Wilson, William Scott. *Ideals of the Samurai: Writings of Japanese Warriors.* Burbank: Ohara Publications, 1982.

Yagyu, Munenori. "Heiho Kadensho." In *The Sword and the Mind* by Sato Hiroaki.

Yamamoto, Tsunetomo. Hagakure: *The Book of the Samurai.* Translated by William Scott Wilson. New York: Kodansha International, 1979.

Yoshikawa, Eiji. *Musashi.* New York: Harper and Row/ Kodansha International, 1981.

The "weathermark" identifies this book as a production of Weatherhill, Inc., publishers of fine books on Asia and the Pacific. Editorial supervision: Ray Furse. Book design: Liz Tovato. Page composition: Charles Clough. Production supervision: Bill Rose. Printing and binding: R. R. Donnelley. The typeface used is Garamond.